THE RECOVERY OF
AMERICAN EDUCATION
Reclaiming a Vision

Edited by

Stephen M. Krason

UNIVERSITY
PRESS OF
AMERICA

Lanham • New York

Copyright © 1991 by Stephen M. Krason

University Press of America®, Inc.
4720 Boston Way
Lanham, Maryland 20706

Library of Congress Cataloging-in-Publication Data

The Recovery of American education : reclaiming a vision
/ edited by Stephen M. Krason.
p.   cm.
Includes bibliographical references and index.
1. Education—United States.   2. Education, Humanistic—United
States.   3. Education—United States—Aims and objectives.
4. Education—United States—Philosophy.   I. Krason, Stephen M.
LA209.2.R39   1991
370'.973—dc20   90–27573 CIP

ISBN 0–8191–8124–2 (alk. paper)
ISBN 0–8191–8125–0 (pbk. : alk. paper)

COPYRIGHT PERMISSIONS

CONTENTS

CONTENTS

PREFACE

Richard M. Weaver once said: "A people does not enjoy a republic, at least for very long, unless the idea of a republic is somewhere forcefully expressed in its culture and similarly ideas of justice and of law spring from the general cultural consciousness."* That a republican government and its characteristic devotion to justice and the rule of law can only be sustained if its people are deeply committed to it and if the spirit of republicanism animates its whole culture is a belief shared, it seems, by every contributor to this book. Education, after the family and possibly religion, is probably most responsible for shaping the commitment to republicanism and the principle behind it. This, too, is well understood by the contributors and forms the basis for many of the essays and for the general thrust of this book. If education is then crucial for the shaping of good and enlightened citizens and leaders, present and future, in a democratic republic, the current "crisis" in education which we hear so much about may rightly be judged as reflecting a crisis, pending or already upon us, in a republican government as well. I do not hesitate to say that the contributors are acutely aware of this fact and most of the essays seek to address this in one fashion or another.

To simply refocus attention on the fact of the dependence of republican government on sound education is a worthwhile undertaking in

*Weaver, Richard M., "The Role of Education in Shaping Our Society," lecture delivered to the Metropolitan Area Industrial Conference, Chicago, October 25, 1962, printed as a pamphlet by the Intercollegiate Studies Institute.

this era of confusion about *both* education and republicanism. The essays, however, go beyond this to explain why in America we traditionally saw education playing this role, how we have fallen away from it, and what principles should form the basis for an attempt to restore it. They attempt to reemphasize an idea -- an ideal--of education which was part of our earlier American understanding, and which was based, in turn, on an older understanding of education in our Western heritage. The latter was shaped by our religious tradition and the traditions of realism in the philosophy and the common good in political and social matters. This is why we speak about the *recovery* of American education and *reclaiming a vision.*

There are more specific aspects of this general purpose of the book. Among the other points it examines are the nature and purpose of the liberal arts, the major vehicle for carrying out the traditional role of education; the role education plays in building the good political order; the basis for the central role played by parents in traditional education of the young; and the nature of the basic problems with present-day education and how adequately they are being addressed.

Many books are available about education. Thus, any new book, in some sense, must justify itself. I believe this book differs from most others recently written on certain important points. First, its essays explore, variously, the basic philosophical premises which must undergird education, the connection between political philosophy (especially that of democratic government) and education, and the current problems of education. Such a combined philosophical--especially political philosophy-- and empirical approach to education is not commonly found in the same volume, in my experience. Second, the book's general theme of the crucial role of education, traditionally, in sustaining, specifically, the American democratic republic is not often stressed nowadays. Third, it discusses both elementary-secondary and college education; most writing on education will deal with one or the other, but not both. Fourth, much of the literature on education today pays scant attention to our culture's and our political order's traditional, fundamental principles in evaluating education or constructing a theory or proposals about it, much less taking as its starting reference point the nature and purpose of man. These points are the center of this book's concern. And finally, the essays in this book do not focus primarily on specific, often secondary educational problems or ills of the present day--the symptoms--but rather on the underlying causes, which are mostly in the realm of a faulty philosophy undergirding education. This, regrettably, is not done frequently enough, which maybe explains why undesirable and, even, dangerous conditions persist in American education.

On the other hand, this book does not claim to treat either elementary-secondary or college education comprehensively. It also does not examine many important themes or critical current issues in them, nor does it, for the most part, discuss the major current ideas or proposals for changing educational structures or setting up alternative structures or other leading public policy proposals for reform.

The writers of the essays in this book include scholars, professors, educators, college presidents (one of whom is a former high federal government appointive official), a notable elected official, and a member of the most recent presidential commission on education. All have had, in their previous writings, lectures, and/or public activities, a considerable opportunity to reflect on the nature, role, and problems of American education. Their essays are all on topics that they are particularly suited to address. John Agresto and John S. Schmitt speak about the basic problems of education today. Agresto's essay discusses the two fundamental roles of liberal education: helping us function better as thinking people so we can ask intelligent, serious questions about the basic aspects of life--its *radical* dimension--and preserving the heritage of our culture--its *conservative* dimension. Both elements of this educational mission are today generally neglected at all levels. One of the major reasons for this is the misuse by teachers of the great books, which he and several other contributors believe are the preeminent tools of instruction. Like Agresto, Schmitt talks about a basic problem of current education (he says it is *the* most basic problem). (He focuses especially on the elementary-secondary level, but his analysis also applies to college education.) This problem is its flawed premise that reality does not exist independently of the mind and cannot be known with certainty. The result, he tells us, is that the natural wonder of children is dampened and they turn away from the asking of ultimate questions and, for that matter, from the life of serious thought at all to the emotional and ephemeral. The pupil is encouraged to see personal freedom as the highest end, so long his particular assertion of freedom conforms to the prevailing relativistic, egalitarian ethos.

Raphael T. Waters, Rev. J. Donald Monan, S.J., and Russell Kirk speak about the essential elements for a renewal of the liberal arts. Lowenthal does too, but also sketches the roots, historical role, and transformation of the liberal arts. Waters' essay explains why a sound philosophical-ethical analysis, built upon a solid understanding of the nature of man, establishes that the function and right of educating children primarily belongs to their parents. Following from this, he discusses why the state, for the most part, has been unjustified in entering the educational field, to say nothing of monopolizing it, and considers what the proper role of the state should be. He examines the totalitarian, collectivist bent of much of modern education in its suppression of parental rights, and provides the basis for a sound philosophy of education. Monan also gives some perspectives about a philosophy of education, specifically focusing on the aim of the liberal arts. He says that the starting point of the liberal arts must be an overarching understanding of the human person--including his ends or purposes--which transcends the confines of the individual disciplines. It is essential, he insists, that a liberal arts education include a study of those arts which are necessary to truly fulfill and enrich the human person so as to enable him to make sound choices in the various areas of human endeavor. There can be no philosophy of liberal arts education, then, if there is no philosophy of the human person to shape it. Monan puts forth the philosophy of the human person as a potential unifying, organizing principle for a liberal arts education comprised of disparate disciplines. Russell Kirk, an eminent American scholar, man of letters, and commentator on education, contributes the first of several essays in this collection that focus on the various purposes of liberal education in the American tradition. He speaks about education having the important task of transmitting the highest elements of our cultural heritage to the next generation. He addresses the question of what is the culture American education should be trying to transmit, and concludes that it is *Christian* culture. Whether one accepts this culture or dissents from it or whether or not one is a Christian does not change the fact that Christianity influenced all areas of life in the history of Europe and America. This is really the substance of what we call "Western culture," and it is what, until recently, Western education sought to transmit. This education endeavored to inculcate a received body of truths which was the basis for the order of the soul, and thence the order of the commonwealth. So, it shaped moral conduct by means of the development of intellectual virtue. Further, he says, knowing our cultural heritage helps us avoid slipping into an orientation of pragmatism. Lowenthal's essay picks up on the theme of education being geared to shaping morality. Rooted in Aristotle, the liberal arts tradition sought to emphasize the practical as well as the theoretical, and one dimension of this was the developing of the (morally) good man. Another was the fashioning of the good citizen. The concomitant education of the good man and the good citizen meant that while civic education was being given--which will be part of education in any political order, because a political order wants to be sure to prepare its youth for future citizenship-- its destructive tendencies would be ameliorated by the shaping of its subjects in virtue (i.e., the education of the good man). Virtue, of course, involved what was good for all men, and so potentially enabled them to develop in the good life beyond what would probably be expected by their political orders. All political orders are imperfect in the sense that they do not measure up to the highest standards of virtue. Thus, civic education (the education of the good citizen), by itself, would not shape the young in great virtue. By shaping the individual in goodness, moral education-- education in virtue--would have the ultimate effect of helping the political order become less imperfect. The good citizen would come to be identified more with the good man. Lowenthal rightfully laments that this vision of education is now gone. In the present day, we have an education which seeks to develop neither the good man nor the good citizen; it is little more than a narrow vocational or technical training which regards no knowledge except that of the natural sciences as truly valid. Like most of the contributors, however, he is hopeful: we have this legacy of the old liberal arts education to guide our future educational enterprises and we have books, especially the great ones, which are great educators.

Christopher Bruell and William M. Bulger speak about education as a preparation for different roles in the political order. Like Lowenthal, Bruell emphasizes that even though they are intimately connected, liberal education is not the same thing as education for citizenship. Even in a good regime, there will be tensions between the two. Apart from even the differing emphases that Lowenthal says were a part of traditional liberal education, Bruell tells us that there are such further problems in its helping to shape good citizens as the fact that attitudes about one's country will be shaped before he is even exposed to education and it may not be able to adequately shape the vital political virtue of prudence. He contends, however, that it can foster the habits of observation and reflection that are integral elements of prudence. It can also help combat false opinions which stand in the way of prudential judgment. A significant part of his discussion is built on the ideas of Thucydides. In the case of the American democratic republic, he tells us that it is vital that its education prepare young people for good citizenship. Bulger speaks about liberal education as preparing a man for one particularly important citizenship role that few attain, serving in public office. He speaks as a man who has had a successful public career, and explains in an eloquent and sagacious way--very impressively for a man whose vocation is in the realm of practical affairs and not scholarship--how his liberal education helped him to prepare for that career. He especially notes the influence the reading of Demosthenes had on him.

Ralph Lerner, Peter V. Sampo, and Richard H. Powers discuss the role of education in the tradition and history of the American political order, specifically. Lerner addresses the views of America's Founding Fathers about education. He focuses specifically on the views of John Adams, a schoolmaster before entering political life. Adams' thought stressed the theme of education being closely tied up with liberty; it was an important factor in making people capable of self-government. He insisted that political participation itself was an educative force and helped in the establishment of a good and free government. He cautioned, however, that education sometimes can be more dangerous than beneficial, especially if it is devoid of a concern with developing character. Further, Adams said we cannot count on it alone to preserve liberty; good institutions will also especially be needed for this. Sampo's thoughtful essay ranges from a discussion of the nature and problems of liberal arts education to the role of education in a commercial republic like the United States. He, like many of the contributors, emphasizes that traditional Western education runs against many modern intellectual currents. American education was squarely in the liberal arts tradition. The American political tradition was oriented to maintaining political liberty and this required freedom for factions to operate (e.g., Federalist 10). It held that, in a roundabout way, this results in the promotion of justice and the general good. Although the very nature of our political institutions encourages this result, education, especially of our leaders, is also necessary. The type of education that was understood as best performing this function is liberal education, for the same reasons that Lowenthal stated (i.e., it trains both the man and the citizen). The problem, Sampo tells us, with liberal education is that is must always be "renewed," and the renewal must be built around the notion that the time used for education is a kind of sacred time in which the student puts aside commercial and other mundane pursuits to turn his attention to seeking the truth. The liberal arts, he insists, demand a total devotion to the truth, even to the point of loving it and sacrificing for it. Two important points he makes about a truly sound liberal education are that it must seek to stimulate the moral imagination (which means that a liberal arts curriculum must include literature as an essential feature and not just be built around philosophy) and that the full human vision that the liberal arts aims to promote--the essential theme of Monan--requires religious faith. Its purpose cannot be achieved by the unassisted, inquiring intellect alone. Powers provides a historical sketch of American schooling since the Founding Fathers' time. He explains how the traditional liberal arts and solid academic standards were undermined in the secondary schools; he says that this happened because of the egalitarian demands of democratic society. He singles out educational innovations in the public schools in our history for special criticism. They have typically appealed to mass tastes, in opposition to the discipline that excellence demands. Speaking about American higher education, he, like most of the contributors, laments the fact that since the nineteenth century it has focused almost exclusively on knowledge instead of wisdom, as previous higher education had done. It also no longer sought to transmit "higher culture" (i.e., the greatest elements of our Western cultural heritage). He also offers this blunt recommendation for restoring both true standards and the integrity of the liberal arts in colleges and universities (at least private ones): bring outside pressure on them through their boards of trustees.

Annette Kirk and Lawrence A. Uzzell assess recent efforts at elementary and secondary school reform and my essay provides a perspective on reforming college and university education. Mrs. Kirk provides a brief reflection on *A Nation at Risk*, the 1983 report of the National Commission on Excellence in Education, of which she was a member. She seems to believe that the report stimulated some serious educational reforms. One important point it stressed is the need to develop the right attitudes in the student if education is to be effective. Another was that the basic cause for the decline of educational standards was the lack of purpose in education. The moral corruption in the schools resulted from a moral vacuum in the character of our education, she says, and illustrates the need to return to a stress on the old, traditional virtues. She laments that the Commission was never able to address how this should be done, but proposes a couple of interesting ideas on her own. Uzzell is not as positive as Annette Kirk about the putative successes which have been achieved in the last few years in American elementary and secondary education. This is seen in his blunt choice of a title: "Elementary and Secondary School Reform: Why It Failed." Unlike many of the other contributors, he seems to see the effect of elementary and secondary education on higher education as more significant than the effect of the latter on the former. He is equally blunt about the reasons for the failure of the "reform movement": it has been controlled by the very public school establishment that needs to be reformed. He discusses a number of assumptions that have animated the thinking of these "reformers" and explains why they are completely erroneous. He concludes that, from the standpoint of the present, the reform movement appears to have done more harm than good. My essay, the last in the volume, speaks about the idea of a "democracy of worth" and how university education in such a democracy--since it is so essential to its preservation--should be structured in order to be compatible with it. There are several questions that must be considered if we are concerned about this problem: Are universities more likely to fit this mold if they are state or privately-controlled? If they are secular or religiously-affiliated institutions? How does the curriculum have to be structured? What should the character of teaching be in a university if its education is to be fit for a "democracy of worth"? How much attention must be given to student discipline and the shaping of good moral character? In such a democracy, who needs and should receive a higher education?

Most of the papers in this book were originally given, some in an earlier form, at a symposium on "Educating the Man and the Citizen in America" at Boston College in Chestnut Hill, Massachusetts on March 29-30, 1985, sponsored by the Intercollegiate Studies Institute (ISI). It was a logical undertaking for ISI, a central part of whose focus for the generation or so of its existence has been preserving the integrity of the liberal arts.

I wish to thank ISI, both for its support of the original symposium and its financial support for the publication of this book. I also thank Franciscan University of Steubenville for financial and other assistance. Additional thanks are due to the following: Dr. David Lowenthal, co-organizer of the 1985 symposium with me, and the conference office at Boston College; Mrs. Pat Mangano, my former secretary at ISI; Mrs. B.J. Brehm of the secretarial staff at Franciscan University of Steubenville for an excellent job of typing the final publication copy of the manuscript for me, Jeffrey Di Bacco for his computer assistance and work on printing the manuscript, Mrs. Katrina Zeno for her proofreading, Nicholas Scarpone and Patrick W. Baker for their help with the Index, and my Department Chairman, Professor Jack R. Boyde. Finally, as always, I wish to acknowledge the strong and loving support of my wife, Therese C. Krason, for this and my many efforts.

Stephen M. Krason
Steubenville, Ohio
June 5, 1990

THE FAILURE OF AMERICAN EDUCATION AS BOTH A RADICAL AND A CONSERVATIVE ENTERPRISE

by John Agresto

The Athenians who killed Socrates were on to something. They knew Socrates was a dangerous man. They knew that this old, streetcorner pest was a moral and social problem. Why? Because everything he said led to one conclusion: Philosophers should rule. Philosophers should be kings. We, of course, say that he believed that philosophers should be kings because he was a philosopher. If he were a grocer, he would probably say grocers should be kings.

So we tend to shrug, and pass it off as a self-serving statement on Socrates' part and a dumb act on the part of the Athenians. Besides, we've met people who call themselves philosophers--and they're usually not worth either crowning or killing.

But the Athenians were, in their own way, far more clearsighted than we. They never, even for a moment, thought that Socrates--or any philosopher--would literally rule over them. He had only a few followers and no army. The Athenians knew, however, that he was not saying that he, Socrates the philosopher, would someday rule them, but that philosophy should govern them--that reasoned informed knowledge should govern their acts and our acts.

Put that way, Socrates' message sounds neither silly nor self-serving.

1

What else besides reasoned, informed knowledge, would direct us? Still, if it's so unexceptional, why did the Athenians feel compelled to kill this old man? Why did the Athenians think that philosophy governing us was so horrible an idea? Let us consider for a moment the alternatives to philosophy ruling. What (besides ignorance, which has few active partisans), is the alternative to knowledge ruling? Who or what has other claims on us?

Well, the first thing the Athenians knew was that to say knowledge and inquiry should govern is to say that our parents, or the wisdom of our ancestors, or today's opinions, maybe shouldn't govern. If we want to act on the basis of reasoned knowledge we've already said that what our friends and our parents thought was right might not be right.

What else has claims on us? Religion--what the priests tell us the mysterious gods want us to do. That, too, will tell us how we should live. The rich and powerful might also think they have claims. But Socrates taught us to ask all of these forces--parents, friends, ancestors, priests, the powerful--to ask all of these people to make an account of themselves before we will listen. To say that informed knowledge should rule was, to the Athenians, an irreverent, impious, nasty, ungrateful, and above all, radical thing to do. It promised to turn over the whole order of society as they knew it and liked it. So they executed him.

Obviously, education at its best is meant to do some of what Socrates asked philosophy to do: it asks us to ask *why*. It wants us not to be satisfied with opinion--you don't have to go to school to learn opinions--but to act upon the best informed judgment you can obtain.

Let me break this down a bit: To study history is to imply that maybe our parents didn't tell us everything; to study philosophy is to suggest that the holy legends and the holy men might have left something out; to study science is to say that even the obvious may not be the whole truth; to study literature is to say that maybe our tribe or our race or our people might not have experienced everything worth experiencing. We all inherit from Socrates one daring and scary impulse: the desire to know and to be changed by that knowing. Of course, our parents, our priests, and our people might in fact have told us the truth. But when we ask to be educated--especially when we study the liberal arts--we begin by saying: First I'll check that out. (On this level, the interesting thing is not that parents encourage such an education but that they even allow such an education.)

The endeavor is even more radical than one might suspect. Let us consider the questions that a true education asks us to confront:

> What can I know?
> What may I hope?

2

> What deserves to be loved?
> What deserves to be hated?
> What does it mean to be just?

Some questions come from philosophy and political science:

> What does a person owe himself or herself?
> What do we owe our countrymen?
> What is the difference between right and power?

From science:

> What are causes? What are effects?
> What makes things what they are?

From history:

> Who was great? Who was false?
> How do societies live and grow and die?
> What of man endures?

From literature:

> What is noble?
> What does it mean to be base?
> What is the proper relation between men and women?
> Why do people fail in their dreams?
> What are fear, courage, fidelity, honor, friendship?
> Why, in God's name, did Cordelia have to die?

But more. As former Secretary of Education William Bennett has said, "We should want every student to know how mountains are made, and that for most actions there is an equal and opposite reaction. They should know who said 'I am the state,' and who said 'I have a dream.' They should know about subjects and predicates, about isosceles triangles and ellipses. They should know where the Amazon flows, and what the First Amendment means. They should know about the Donner Party, and slavery, and Shylock, Hercules, and Abigail Adams, where Ethiopia is, and why there is [was] a Berlin Wall. They should know a little of how a poem works, and what 'If wishes were horses beggars would ride' means. They should know something about the Convention of 1787 and about the conventions of good behavior. They should know a little of what the Sistine Chapel looks like and what great music sounds like."

That is the level of the enterprise. When we ask, what does it mean to be educated, that is what we mean. When we know some literature, the world will not so much surprise us. When we know philosophy we may not be swayed by so many bad arguments. When we study history, we will, one hopes, know something of who we are, and why. We will not be seduced by every trend or scandalized by what passes for change in this world. To be governed by the knowledge of these things is an absolutely radical, transforming activity.

But this radicalism is only half of what a true education does. The other half is very conservative. Or, at least, it should be. Every decent education necessarily serves the function of preserving. Only through education can we preserve and then transmit the story of Job, or Jefferson, or Beethoven, or the Parthenon.

Socrates had to begin from scratch. We don't. We have books. In fact, to be honest about it, we have the best books. We have Shakespeare, and Dante, and the Bible. We have Homer and Tolstoy. We have Twain, and Dickens, and George Eliot, and the Brontes, and Jefferson. We have not only the radical questions but, paradoxically, the tradition of radical, deep, penetrating, different answers. Liberal education means turning from our real parents and finding new parents--new answer-givers, answer-proposers--in books. Liberal education means the conservation and transmission of two millennia of radical questions and penetrating answers. If students come to college and do not learn those books, they have been cheated. No matter how advanced their opinions, no matter how far on the cutting edge of scholarship they are, if students leave college without knowing some of these books--many of these books--they were had.

Thus, a true liberal education has both a radical side and a conservative side. It asks the most important questions and it offers to us 2,000 years of great texts trying to answer those questions. The crisis in liberal education comes when we overlook those questions and when we hesitate or refuse to transmit the legacy.

So let us ask the current $64,000 question: If we pretend to be the heirs of Socrates, who today are his executioners? Who kills both the liberal and conservative legacy of true education?

Well, the first enemy of liberal education is the teacher who deradicalizes it: who fails to see that education is a transforming experience, that education means to let us be different people than we were before. Here is an example: the National Endowment for the Humanities set up some seminars for high school teachers, each led by a major scholar, and each on a book or related set of books. One of these professors, eminent in the world of scholarship, wanted to teach the book he knew best. When he sent us his syllabus it was filled with secondary readings, biographies of the author, articles on abstruse points the professor had written--and excerpts from the book--the book they were to be studying as a class. When we told him that all the paraphernalia of scholarship was overtaking the text--that he should concentrate on the great book--he looked at us blankly: "But after we read it, what will we do to it?" It never dawned on him that one does not do something to great books--that they were written to do something to us. Yet half the professors we talked to had no idea what it meant to be transformed--educated--by a book: books, they thought, existed to do things to, as if they were crossword puzzles, or trivia games. They think scholarship is not learning from texts with students, but, rather, each professor taking in another professor's laundry. The first executioners of true education are those who suppose that education means learning about books instead of from books.

This same idea was said much better elsewhere:

> Only the learned read old books, and we have now so dealt with the learned that they are of all men the least likely to acquire wisdom by doing so. We have done this by inculcating the Historical Point of View. The Historical Point of View, put briefly, means that when a learned man is presented with any statement in an ancient author, the one question he never asks is whether it is true. He asks who influenced the ancient writer, and how far the statement is consistent with what he said in other books, and what phase in the writer's development, or in the general history of thought, it illustrates, and how it affected later writers, and how often it has been misunderstood (especially by the learned man's own colleagues) and what the general course of criticism on it has been for the last ten years, and what is "the present state of the question." To regard the ancient writer as a possible source of knowledge--to anticipate that what he said could possibly modify your thoughts or your behavior--this would be rejected as unutterably simple-minded.

--C.S. Lewis, *The Screwtape Letters*, pp. 128-129.

This leads directly to my second point: The second crisis in contemporary education comes with the "ideologization"--the sometimes blatant, sometimes subtle--politicization of study. I mean here all the "isms" and "ologies" through which we sometimes wrongly think it smart to filter our studies. I mean here the varieties of Determinism, Reductionism, Historicism, and any number of other "isms" which, in some areas are informative, maybe even true, but in the education of students--especially in the humanities--are generally distorting. I mean to include in this even that great love of all undergraduates--the putting of things "in historical context."

Nothing makes us feel smarter, and leaves us less satisfied, than the desire to see things in context, in their times, or to be content to trace their lineage--whether it be sociological, historical, or psychological. A great book put in historical perspective distances that book from us and is another way of only learning about books, not from them. We learn next to nothing from our legacy when we reduce our books to their circumstances or to historical/biographical/psychological causality.

Strange to say, I'm talking here about the humanities part of higher education and not the social science or natural science part. Consider this: When a student in physics class asks a professor, "Why did Einstein say $E=mc^2$?" he is given reasons. He is not told "Because Einstein reflected the general spirit of his times," or "Because of his early childhood," or "Because he came from a race or family noted for its love of science." Rather than causes, the student is given reasons. How different it often is in the humanities, the home of reasons. When the same student asks his humanities professor why Aristotle believed "x" or Shakespeare said "y" or Luther did "z," he is often told such gems as "Well, Aristotle was a Greek, and the Greeks considered themselves superior to their neighbors" or "We have to understand the context in which Shakespeare wrote and the fact that he had Elizabethan notions" or "We have to know about Luther's relationship to his father and that he had stomach trouble." Having reduced all ideas to their "context" and having given causes rather than reasons, we no longer explain thoughts, we explain them away. We become smug and smart rather than thoughtful or intelligent. Again, rather than learn from books and authors, the newer way is to learn about them. The truth is we would not think of treating even ourselves the way we treat our books.

However, in many places the deepest crisis of liberal education has to do not with the decline of education's radical mission but with its "conservative" mission.

The greatest scandal of higher education lies in the fact that in many places college students can graduate and know next to nothing about the civilization of which they are members. I mean--to be blunt--that they can graduate and be ignorant of what we can only call Western Civilization. A student today can earn a bachelor's degree from 75 percent of all American colleges and universities without having studied European history, from 72 percent without having studied either American literature or American history, and from 86 percent without having studied the civilizations of Greece and Rome. When one of my colleagues recently asked a third-year law class at a prestigious private law school how many of them had ever read any of the *Federalist Papers*, the number, out of 25 students, was zero. As the National Endowment for the Humanities wrote in *To Reclaim a Legacy,* "although more than 50 percent of American high school graduates continue their education at American colleges and universities, few of them can be said to receive there an adequate education in the culture and civilization of which they are members. We, the educators, have too often given up the great task of transmitting a culture to its rightful heirs. What we have on many of our campuses is an unclaimed legacy."

We are not born civilized: every civilization is only one generation deep. If the heritage of the past is not transmitted and retained, it is lost. If we

6

lose the legacy, we lose it; and the work of thousands of minds is shot.

As Walter Lippmann once said, "What enables us to know more than our ancestors is that we start with a knowledge of what our ancestors have already learned." We think it wrong so to corrupt developing societies with Western ways that they lose the heritage of their culture, their acquired wisdom. In the same vein, American colleges and universities should have an obligation to preserve and transmit this culture: they have no right to be agents of cultural suicide.

I do not mean only to single out colleges and universities. Our high schools, which were our first line of defense against cultural and intellectual disintegration, are now in shambles. Three years ago, when I was teaching at a major southeastern university, I asked freshmen honors students a set of twenty general knowledge questions: In what town was Christ born? Who wrote *Moby Dick*? Name three of Shakespeare's plays. Who was president immediately preceding Eisenhower? These were hardly "trivia" questions. High school graduates should be expected to have at least a passing familiarity with the landmarks of their culture. Still, more than half the students answered more than half the questions wrong. The heritage of this--or any--culture seemed to mean nothing to them. They were born yesterday and proud of it. They had learned next to nothing in high school.

Yet it was more than merely the imitation of collegiate sophistication that caused high schools to abandon the desire to instill some thoughtfulness and civic learning in students. In some quarters a philosophy of pre-collegiate education took hold that consciously rejected the old "academic" view of schooling. When former President Reagan, in one his addresses on education, held up for rejection the idea that students could earn academic credit for courses such as cheerleading and bachelor living, he was chided in print by one of our local school superintendents. Although cheerleading might be suspect, we were told, bachelor living was a "life skill." The thought that schools might be for something other, and higher, than the transmission of daily competencies is, clearly, not universally shared. Until fairly recently, for example, the only courses required for graduation from Illinois high schools were P.E. and driver training. And one of my young friends told me a few years ago that she could earn one credit in her high school just by taking a course in weight-watching. When we lose sight of what schools are for, it becomes hard to make them better.

High schools should not prepare students for college by trying to mimic the sophistication of collegiate life, with its specialized courses and its myriad of electives. It is there, in the high schools, where we have always expected the basic transmission of this culture to take place; there, where our children would first read the basic books and repeat to themselves the first stories of civilization.

But high schools take their cue from colleges. If a significant number of

American colleges were to say loudly and publicly, that they will not consider for admission any student who had not read some Shakespeare or Homer, who did not know the Bible, or who had not read the Declaration of Independence, or the Constitution, high schools would fall over each other in a rush to adapt.

So these are the questions students must ask:

---First. Am I being exposed to the best that has ever been thought and said? Do I know what the best minds have to offer?
---Second. Am I learning *from* these great books, great events, and great men--or only *about* them.
---Third. Can I truly say that my education has made me a shareholder in my culture, that my inheritance was at least offered to me?

If students and faculty can say "yes" to all three questions, there's no problem. If they say "no" to any one of them, the crisis is at hand.

THEY NO LONGER ASK THE BIG QUESTIONS

by John S. Schmitt

The American schools have come in for much criticism. We are told that the schools are not meeting society's needs let alone the needs of pupils in matters of literacy, marketable job skills, citizenship and equity.

We have been told that the schools' contribution to American prosperity, security and civility is seriously failing and that we are a nation at risk.[1]

Where have we gone wrong? Despite the fact that the schools in a democracy cannot but reflect society's mores and ethos, we still hear criticism. Despite the fact that the schools have had at their disposal, for generations now, the very best expertise, analysis and recommendations of practitioners and professionals whose very business it is to assure sound American education--despite this--we still hear criticism. Where have we gone wrong?

I wish to suggest that the real cause for dissatisfaction should not be falling test scores, unemployability, even relative illiteracy or violence in the corridors. We must be concerned and do all we can to alleviate these problems. The real cause of dissatisfaction, however, is without doubt much more profound, and the problems I have mentioned are, perhaps, but remote symptoms.

Let me give you an analogy to help me communicate what I have to say. Inferential or deductive thinking concludes from premises. If the conclusion is wrong, then we must look either to the premises or to the

9

logical process.

Now I suggest that the critics and the professional improvers have almost completely addressed themselves to the process of education while paying scant attention to the premises that really matter. The professional educators and administrators have been working within the system's parameters adjusting this, tuning that. Albert Jay Nock, that superfluous man, has characterized it:

> Our system has been subjected to incessant
> tinkering...all this tinkering has been purely
> mechanical and external...We have scrapped
> one piece of curricular machinery after another
> and introduced new ones.[2]

A few of these expedients come to mind: language labs, project method, hands-on, resource centers, media centers, new math, computer skills. Much of this has been advantageous to the student, if not the teacher, particularly in relieving dull routine and mechanical activity. Yet with all this expertise and merchandise, we still seem to be unsatisfied with the outcome.

To be sure, there is much to be done to improve the process. I know from years of experience that much of what the Paideia Program proposes in content and method, if implemented, would improve the process. But the real problem in American education is in the premises.

There are, of course, many premises in such a vast and complex undertaking as American education. Many of these premises are unique, democratic and praiseworthy. One, for example, is the idea that the family, the church, the community and the school are to be partners in the education of the young. Another is that every young person is to be given an equal opportunity to reach his or her capacity of excellence.

But there are other premises not of a sociological, political or economic nature that must be reassessed.

Issues that matter in anything including education are rooted in deeper premises in philosophy and ultimately in the way we see reality and those larger questions, and answers, which the humanities, liberal arts and liberal studies and ultimately religion are really about: the ultimate concerns of all people everywhere that must not only be addressed but also answered. I say this even though I know that there are those who see no practical utility in thinking--thinking about matters philosophical--any more than the incontinent want to talk about chastity.

There are many philosophical premises worth examining, but it seems to me that all questions come down at last to the philosophical first principle that reality does exist independently of the mind and that it can be known with certainty.

However, the most basic premise increasingly taken for granted by both the educated community and the larger society, explicitly and implicitly and therefore the more effectively communicated by the university, the colleges and the schools, is the denial that the mind can with certainty know reality.

This fundamental skepticism kills wonder and substitutes curiosity, frustrates hopeful striving for transcendence, and turns the young pupil toward the ephemeral, the emotional, the secular, the immediate and the mundane. Our pupils shun the delights of the mind, the humanities, the liberal arts and studies, and in their stead, they seek meaning in the practical and professional arts that pay more obvious rewards.

Besides all this, fundamental skepticism is not an option. Reality is real and it exists independently of our perceptions of it. It can be known, within limits, of course. But it is certainly known, and we can make judgments and statements, act on it, and make works of art regarding it, which statements we can know to be true or false, good or bad, beautiful or ugly, or something between.

Unless this basic orientation to reality be recognized and communicated, intelligence and true liberal education is impoverished, falters and finally becomes meaningless.

If we tell our pupils there is no final answer or truth in reality regarding their wonder about larger questions of destiny, life and death, of human nature and ultimate reality itself; if we cut off their queries by telling them that there are only variations of considered opinion, why should they think that one opinion is better than another?

If the schools are not about truth--always about truth--it's a fair question to ask, what are we doing? That question is not lost on youth. They assign the humanities, where at least some of these questions are searched out and answered, to the eggheads, and then the students get going on more meaningful career courses or job training.

If we tell our pupils that all values and principles of moral and ethical behavior are situationally, socially or subjectively determined, why should we be surprised that they do not meet our expectations? Aren't we all doing our own thing, which, incidentally, looks mighty like what everybody else is doing?

If we tell our pupils that "beauty is only in the eye of the beholder," or only a matter of feeling and emotion, why should they listen to Mozart rather than the latest pop-rock whose themes seem invariably to be violence, eroticism and sentimental self-pity? Or why should they gaze for even a

11

moment of wonder at the gloriously setting sun, with its subtly nuanced epic, lyric and dramatic rhythms of motion and color when they can stare for five hours a day at a box that plugs into a wall socket?

The secondary school years are the critical years in the development of the intellectual life that is at the center of liberal education.

As young boys and girls come up through the grades into the secondary school, they experience a gradual deadening of wonder. Wonder marks all learning and childhood as it stands before what is, before real things. Wonder leads through reverence and piety to knowledge, and with courage and counsel on to understanding and wisdom which is the satisfaction of wonder. Children naturally know that the realm of knowledge and truth is based on underived primary principles animated by wonder. This they do not doubt. This they take for granted even though they are unable to articulate it in their innocence. They know too that there are real answers out there to be searched out and discovered.

When they leave us to go on to higher education, the job-market or whatever, very few seem to wonder any longer. They no longer ask the big questions. They have learned not to be so naive. For they have learned in their English, history and reductionist psychology classes that there is no ultimate reality to be known; only fact and opinion. They are told that the claims of objective reality lead to unacceptable things like dogmatism, authoritarianism and intolerance. They are told that they must learn to cope with uncertainty and ambiguity in an evolving and progressing world. They are told that their education is a great ongoing search, a quest for personal and social significance and meaning, whatever that may mean. There is some truth in all this doxa, to be sure.

For most, there is very little summoning and awakening into the intellectual life. For most, schooling is a rather passive acquiescence into the socially dominant logos, pathos and ethos. Very many never are able to connect their practical living experiences with much intellectual understanding, and the realm of the mind is left pretty much undisturbed. These boys and girls remain for the most part on the level of sense experience. The significance of truth, goodness and beauty is grasped solely in their feelings and emotions. Most of these pupils are passed on through the grades with maturation effecting more of a change than the efforts of teachers. Education to them is training in marketable basic skills, and these young people become the solid, sturdy yeomen of every culture.

But there are others of a more academic cast of mind. We call them brighter pupils who have promise! They soon enough learn that philosophy, that is love of wisdom, is not a way of life but a college major which has to do with epistemological word games for those who like that sort of thing. As for their grasp of reality and truth, well, truth is a construct of the mind itself and not a discovery of anything out there to which one must conform and be informed by. Each person must invent and fashion his construct for himself as long as it is egalitarian, liberal, pro-science, anti-authoritarian and secular, and, of course, conforms with socially acceptable values of behavior.

These young people lose their wondering innocence and intellectual humility that make all learning possible. In their place is substituted an artificial and sophisticated hubris. In another slightly different context, applicable here, William Bennett has written:

> There is no longer agreement on the value
> of historical facts, empirical evidence, or
> even rationality itself.[3]

The intellectual authority of objective and common sense realism has been replaced with the authority of subjectivity and relativism. The unexamined life of the intellect is indifferently set aside for more "meaningful" experiences. Reason is disconnected from truth, morality from reason. Virtue is confused with emotions and feelings, ends with means. These young people are subject to a peculiar perversion which Plato identified as Sophistry. Truth is no longer the mistress of the schools, no longer pursued and embraced.

What is pursued by these young people of promise in the best tradition of Sophist Athens are the professions. The professions offer exclusive technical know-how and challenge as well as all the material amenities that success can bring.

I must tread lightly here because we all know exceptions to this rather dismal picture. We know individual young men and women with whom we have had the privilege of working who, swimming against the tide of so much of the contemporary youth culture, are our personal student heroes in a way we admire. Not all mechanics, doctors, clerks and attorneys belong to the firm of Solitary, Nasty, Brutish and Short.

And yet the disquieting shortcomings of our education are there. Why else this plethora of studies and reports, books and seminars across the land?

Let me give you some finding of nearly 1,500 individual interviews conducted at twenty of what might be called prestigious eastern and midwestern colleges. I refer to a small publication of the Association for Cultural Interchange by Dr. John Gueguen, Professor of Political Science at Illinois State University. He writes:

> These young people see their present lives and future
> goals in a self-centered light...the personal growth
> they hope to achieve...is oriented toward self-
> development and self-gratification....a majority admit

13

to being uncertain about the values that inform and transcend their immediate objectives, and even wonder whether it is possible to secure them...[they] realize only faintly the connection between what they hold to be true and how they conduct their lives...[they] find questions of truth and other permanent realities quite remote from their thoughts, often lacking even desire to get to the bottom of things, suspecting that truth is merely a matter of opinion without universality or even authenticity...[they] resist the idea that there are authentic transcendent values and resent any effort to espouse such values as an infringement upon their freedom and an affront to their autonomy.

Most confuse freedom with spontaneity or independence and make their lives a display of utilitarian pursuits on the way to material success. Very few seem to realize that they are victimized by the heavy overlay of an ideology which conceals the authentic promptings of reason and misdirects man's natural desire for truth and happiness...The university seems to be just another social agency which more or less directly reinforces the prevailing goals and values...At most the contemporary university in the United States provides a benign context within which any individual is free to pursue his own goals.[4]

In conclusion, I wish to say, that as the colleges and the universities go regarding the love of truth, goodness and beauty, so will go the schools. When higher education puts its own house in order intellectually, then we can look for better education in our schools, for the American educational enterprise is increasingly a 16-year curriculum with more and more young people aspiring to higher education. What is more, our teachers on the secondary level are college educated and university trained.

The work and leisure that is education has to do with the grand panorama of knowable reality and not the great stereopticon of flickering shadows, reflections and opinions. Too many of our young are being entertained on the benches of the cave where they sit chained collectively indifferent to truth. Their lives reflect cognitive and ethical relativism and the subjectivity of truth and values.

We who have glimpsed the truth must lead as Virgil led his pupil, Dante, up that difficult path to the light:

My guide and I came on that hidden road to make our way back into the bright world; and with no care for any rest, we climbed--he first, I following--until I saw, through a round opening, some of those things of beauty heaven bears. It was from there that we emerged, to see--once more--the stars.[5]

NOTES

1. The National Commission on Excellence in Education, *A Nation at Risk: The Imperative for Educational Reform,* U.S. Department of Education, April, 1983.

2. Albert Jay Nock, *The Theory of Education in the United States* (Chicago: Henry Regnery Company, 1949), p. 35.

3. William J. Bennett, "To Reclaim a Legacy," *The Chronicle of Higher Education,* Nov. 28, 1984, p. 19.

4. John A. Gueguen, *Knowledge and the Meaning of Man in the University Today* (New York: Association for Cultural Interchange, Inc., 1981), p.3.

5. Dante Allighieri, *The Divine Comedy of Dante Allighieri, Inferno,* Trans. Allen Mandlebaum (New York: Bantam Books, Inc., 1982), p. 317.

VALUES AND RIGHTS IN EDUCATION

by Raphael T. Waters

INTRODUCTION

There is an undeniable assault upon parental authority in the contemporary scene and none more so than in the field of education. We are witness to the gradual erosion of the rights of those who have brought children into the world and are charged with the responsibility of ensuring that their offspring receive the education which is due to man inasmuch as he is a rational animal. For man is a complex production of nature and requires physical, intellectual and moral education in order to complete the task of preparing new members of the human species.

"Go forth and multiply" was the divine command but the philosopher, viewing human nature from a purely rational perspective, understands the need for many which is necessary because a few will not suffice. Indeed, many men (both male and female) are needed to manifest all that man can manifest. Moreover, the ancient dictum of the Neoplatonic philosophers allows us to view the divine creative act as one in which "good is diffusive of itself" indeed. It is in keeping with this metaphysical explanation that we must see the education of children.

The responsibility of parents does not end with the birth of a child, for the work has to be completed. The process perfective of the offspring is called "education" and tends toward the completion of the undertaking commenced with conception. Replacing the individual members of our species is an important task and it behoves us to consider well *who* has the responsibility and therefore the right to carry out the task either directly or with the aid of others. The task we refer to as education is vital not only for

17

the individual but also for the due perfection of the social organism in which each individual lives. This inquiry in the contemporary scene is urgent; its outcome could be even more urgent.

PARENTAL AUTHORITY TO NURTURE AND EDUCATE THEIR OWN CHILDREN

Throughout the history of mankind, communities both civilized and uncivilized appear to assume that all responsibility for children belongs to those who gave birth to them. Indeed, the terms, "foster parent," "God-parent," "ward," and a host of others appearing in various languages add credence to the common judgment of members of every community that some *particular* persons are to be preferred and have been accepted as supervisors of the development of children, their growth, their housing, feeding and clothing; more importantly, their *education* has formed the center of attention of those in charge of the offspring. In fact, if the government for any reason had to assume responsibility for some junior members of a family, either, for example, on account of the death of their natural parents or some such, others were delegated wherever possible to replace the parents even if this could only be achieved by means of an orphanage. But no one would question the fact that the biological parents were, by far, the best fitted to nurture and supervise the educational development of children. In other words, adoption was the exception in a world inhabited by families in the true sense of the word, just as surely it is today.

This arrangement of human affairs did not arise as if by accident or without design. For its necessity was readily grasped by the common sense of mankind, that there is a natural order among men just as there is among lower animals, the brutes that act purely instinctively. How easy it is to observe in the behavior of the latter natural inclinations whereby, without any intellectual process or historical influence, those who produce the offspring will house and feed them with great ingenuity, while on the other hand, they will defend them will all the ferocity at their command. Naturalists will marvel at the instinctive "motherly" activities of a robin or female rabbit while puzzling over the apparent neglect of a male crocodile.

Could we expect anything less in man? If nature were to be left to her own designs the reply to that question might very well be in the negative. But man alone can deviate from his nature. Man alone has free will whereby, while claiming to have psychological freedom, he will assert a spurious moral freedom allowing himself license to act against what his nature demands. For, in contrast with other animals which act merely instinctively, man can use his reason to denature himself, that is to say, to act in a manner contrary to his nature; but this nature is the specifying principle which determines the norm of how he ought to act inasmuch as he is a free animal. His nature remains the same whether he wants to rebel against it or not.

In other words, man, who alone is rational, is psychologically free to act contrary to reason. He alone has devised methods whereby his actions constitute an attack on his own kind. Hence, some men find it possible to deny parents their proper responsibility with regard to their own children. This has happened in recent years when some have refused parents the right to bring up and educate their offspring. Indeed, attacks on the family have come from many sides and are based on many facets of family life.[1]

This denial of the due authority of parents is in keeping with the many attempts to submerge the family so noticeable in various departments of human affairs.[2] But the interference with an order well established by nature and so easily discerned by the good common sense of mankind is disastrous. The denial of parental responsibility is perilous to the race as much as it is to the individual person being brought into the world.

The two functions weighing upon parents--attending to the child's physical needs (food, clothing, housing), and his education--must suffer if those whose love forms the environmental setting of his upbringing are not given free reign. Parents alone can love a child sufficiently to allow them to attend to all the daily needs, demands, accidents, difficulties, and doubts of an offspring who resembles his parental guardians inasmuch as he is *their* offspring, *their* continuation, *their* unification or blend of being, resembling *them* in having human nature--*particular* human nature--*their* genes and so on. In short, no one could doubt, generally speaking, whose child it is, and that he is deserving of their special care.

Aristotle notes how essential love is to the formation and continued existence of the family:

> Parents then love their children as themselves, for their issue are by virtue of their separate existence a kind of other selves; children love their parents as being born of them; while brothers love one another as born of the same parents, identity with whom identifies them with one another...those brought up together tend to be comrades.[3]

But he assures us that "parents love their children from the moment the latter are born."[4]

The authority conferred on a couple by nature is easily recognized as a continuum which will be completed only after the offspring has achieved a certain maturity. What happens between his conception and that completion of the process has its foundation in the special inclination and love deeply radicated in the nature of parents. Are they not then the best fitted to attend to the perfecting process of that new member of the human species, that is, his education? Will they not attend more carefully to the maturation of his physical, intellectual, and moral education--that which has been defined as: "Development and advance of the human offspring right up to the perfect state of man forasmuch as he is man, which is the state of virtue?"[5]

The strong tendency to love their own child, found universally among families of every race and every period, manifests something born into the nature of man.[6] For since effects are in the same order or genus as their causes, and a common effect demands a common cause, such a strong tendency belongs to the human race, that is, to man as he is man. A man knows that he has an obligation to rear that child, understanding himself to love and be responsible for that *particular* child; moreover, since nature does nothing in vain, such an obligation has to be met since that is by far the best way to achieve the due perfectioning of the human race. Therefore, since rights are corollaries of obligations, that is, for every obligation we have a consequent right, the parents have the right to educate their own child. Their nature as parents has imposed the obligation and, therefore, they possess a moral power over others (the very meaning of a right) whereby other men are morally obliged to admit the right of those parents to educate their child.[7]

Yet it must be said that if the love of parents for their children is missing, nevertheless the obligation remains, for love is not the principle of education but *perfects* the familial society inasmuch as it fuels the efforts of the conjugal couple as they apply themselves to the daily tasks. In other words, the obligation does not merely spring from the love so that some might construe the above reasoning to suppose that they would be morally free to abandon, or abort, or allow their child to be adopted. On the contrary, notwithstanding the absence of love, parents are obliged to be sure that their own offspring will in some way benefit from the rearing and educative process. It goes without saying, that education does not mean advanced schooling so that parents might feel free to escape their duty of offering their child to another for achieving that end.

Man, with his acts of self-governance[8] has a strong appetite to remove impediments to the exercise of his inner tendencies; in other words, to remove those things which might prevent him from seeking his personal good, satisfying the natural inclinations to obtain those goods which perfect his being. We can compare this with the function of a *physician* whose task it is to help the tendency of the human body heal itself, that is, to obtain that good which is called "health" and which consists in a normal, organic constitution. The physician does not heal the patient; rather the latter heals himself while the physician removes all impediments to the healing process.

In similar manner, *civil authority* does not obtain the common good in a political society but the people, acting cooperatively, obtain the common good; the function of the government is to coordinate the citizens' efforts

20

towards the common good and to remove any impediments to that natural process. It is even clearer that the function of a *teacher* is to coordinate the efforts of the student and to remove any impediment to the process whereby the student educates himself.[9] The latter is the educator and at the same time, is the educated. He does the acts of understanding--no one can do that for him. But a teacher can remove obstacles to understanding by proposing various examples to illustrate the points. Since, in effect, the parents are truly educating an extension of themselves and since, moreover, everything loves its own good,[10] then the parents are best fitted to attend to the important task of developing what, in effect, is *their* own good; thus they carefully oversee the development of their own child.

The whole undertaking, simply expressed, denotes that:

> Education is the prolonging of procreation and its completion. The two form but one and the same function. For procreation is the communicating of the same human life that education aims to develop and unfold.[11]

The patience required for the ongoing, everyday supervision of a son with the eternal hope that he will turn out like his mother and father (and *not* like that other wayward little fellow up the street!) or even better than *they* had every hoped to be, avoiding the multitude of errors *they* made, can be found alone in those who love that child best of all, namely those of whom he is a part--or at least a projection.

The self-governance spoken of above has to be admitted within the domestic unit as well as in civil society and the person.[12] The family can look after its own affairs and civil authority has the heavy obligation of removing any obstacles which might impede it from attending to that duty and attending to it well. Men and women, cooperating within the family unit, are capable of watching over their little ones and attending to their needs while giving special consideration to their individual abilities and disabilities. And love is a strong moving force which spurs the parents along the path of human development; and love is the healing balm when all goes wrong. No one--no teacher, government agent, or other vicarious parent--can love a child as its own parents can love it.[13] The natural tendency is so great that the incidence of a mother or father laying down his or her life for an offspring is not surprising, nor unusual. In the current era, many, through a process of *de-education*, have manifested their capacity for neglecting their own children, but this is not normal--even if it were common--and results from the loss of a well-informed public opinion, one of the supreme common goods of the body politic--and other de-educative influences.

This love accompanies a great urge in the heart of the parent to develop the child; the urge can be satisfied only by achieving the due perfection of the offspring inasmuch as it is perfective of the parents themselves. The principle of reason so well enunciated by the Neoplatonic philosophers when they said that "good is diffusive of itself,"[14] allows us to grasp the importance of this inclination toward perfection. The mother robin by a similar natural appetite, protects her little ones and fights to remove any danger or other impediment to their full development. Everything tends to guard its existence, having a great appetite to maintain its integrity; thus the reproductive urge in living things preserves and perfects the species.[15] Hence it is that parents not only experience within themselves a need to reproduce but they apprehend the product as an extension of themselves as well as a spreading of the goodness of their own being. If an artist will lovingly mold his masterpiece, shouldn't we expect parents to mold their own child with an even greater love? Here one is reminded of parents proudly proclaiming, "That's *my* boy who scored a goal!" or "That's *my* daughter in the front row!"

St. Thomas Aquinas expresses the relation between parent and child with his usual "clearness of thought and precision of style"[16] in the following manner:

> The father is the principle of generation, of education and discipline and of everything that bears upon the perfecting of human life.[17]

Moreover, as he shows:

> The child is naturally something of the father...so by natural right the child, before reaching the use of reason, is under the father's care. Hence, it would be contrary to natural justice if the child, before the use of reason, were removed from the care of the parents.[18]

If one takes adequately into account the psychophysical complexity of human nature, it can be seen that the rearing of a child is an equally complex task. Consider, for example, the following: man's six pleasurable appetites and his five aggressive appetites;[19] their relation to and influence by the four internal senses; the corresponding eleven appetites of the will; the interaction between the intellect, will, internal sense, and eleven passions, not to mention the influence of the external senses and the locomotive power! As if this was not enough, parents have to contend with any one of approximately twelve different temperaments and, to add to the difficulties, inordinate formation of accustomizations which exacerbate fears, angers, or other tendencies. Such a psychophysical organism puts upon a parent the responsibility which can be faced only in a kind of apprenticeship wherein daily contact, guided by natural instincts, and perfected by love, alone suffices to supervise the ongoing process of development and the confrontation with the trials and tribulations of daily living. Facing the joys and sorrows in this "vale of tears" can only be succored with fully sensitive attentiveness by means of the presence of those who offer the safety of a harbor when no one else cares.

If we wish to express what has been written above in arguments defending the rights of parents in education, we can discover a number as follows:

Argument I: From the Natural End of the Domestic Society (the Family)

In his famous treatise on social philosophy, Aristotle sets out the principle of this argument quite clearly when he states that:

> [T]he nature of a thing is its end. For what each thing is when fully developed, we call its nature, whether we are speaking of a man, a horse, or a family. Besides, the final cause and end of a thing is the best, and to be self-sufficing is the end and the best.[20]

This text proposes that the supreme principle in the practical order (i.e., the arena of human actions) concerns the end (i.e., loosely speaking, the purpose) inasmuch as every agent acts for the sake of an end, and as Aristotle puts it, "in actions the final cause is the first principle, as the hypotheses are in mathematics."[21] St. Thomas confirms this understanding of reality, for, as he explains, "the end...is the first principle in all matters of action,"[22] adding elsewhere that, "in things which come to be for the sake of an end, the end holds the same order which the premise [principium] holds in demonstrative sciences."[23] Implicit in the above texts is the fact that this principle applies at every level of human activity, whether in individual actions or group actions. For example, the two natural groups, the domestic society and the political society, exist precisely in order to obtain a common good which is the end or final cause of their existence. The end of the cooperative activity of the members of these two social organisms wherein they achieve their due perfection, provides us with an apt measure of their being and their operations. Hence, since each of these groups consists of a collection of *free*, rational beings, the end provides us with a measure of how they *ought* to operate in order to achieve what is best for them.

While applying this principle to the domestic society, we should note that the fullness of humanity is the due perfection of man and that the family unit exists so that new, live men can be produced and perfected; in other words, that they might arrive at that state wherein man has reached the perfection due to man as man. This is clear from the common sense of mankind, together with a study of the nature of the domestic society, as well as a study of man and woman's physical, physiological and psychological

23

complementarity. St. Thomas, speaking of the "principal end of matrimony," namely, the "good of the offspring," sums up this teaching:

> [N]ature intends not only the begetting of offspring, but also its education and development until it reaches the perfect state of man as man, and that is the state of virtue. Hence, according to the Philosopher [i.e., Aristotle, *N. Ethics* VIII, 11, 12] we derive three things from our parents, namely existence, nourishment, and education.[24]

Education above all brings about the perfective state so desirable in man for this pertains to his higher faculties, those powers separating man from all other bodily things. Nature wants a complete and perfected man, a man who can provide the necessities of life for himself and perhaps, dependents, and above all, can exercise the virtue of prudence in directing his life towards its ultimate end--in sum, a man who is capable of self-governance during the rest of his life. This is a grave responsibility for those who provide those three things, namely "existence, nourishment, and education."

Nature having imposed on the domestic society such a serious obligation, the parents now have rights before other members of human society to recognize that obligation and to allow them all those rights required to carry out their duty; for a right is a corollary of an obligation. We have rights only since we already have obligations.[25]

It is clear, then, that nature is not content with the production of a mere conception but requires that this human biological entity achieve full maturity. For this purpose she has instituted the domestic society which alone is an apt and duly proportioned society for obtaining that maturation of the child.

Aristotle notes that the family has priority of existence over the civil society, for friendship, which is the basis of every society, "seems to exist by nature" between man and wife; he lays the foundation of our argument from the end of the domestic society when he claims that:

> Between man and wife friendship seems to exist by nature; for man is naturally inclined to form couples-- even more than to form cities, inasmuch as the household is earlier and more necessary than the city, and reproduction is more common to man with the animals.[26]

This illuminating text expresses the mind of Aristotle with clarity while laying the foundation of his domestic and political social theory. The following can be drawn from his statement: 1) The domestic society is a natural society--not merely arbitrary; 2) The domestic society exists--at least, in nature--prior to the civil society; 3) Friendship is a common good of the domestic society; 4) The inclination to reproduce is contained in the essence of man, that is, it forms part of human nature; 5) Reproduction has priority of nature over acts of exchange in the body economic and the common goods obtained in the state (city/state); 6) Reproduction is the ultimate reason man is divided into male and female. Other common goods, for example friendship (mutual love), mutual aid, and a natural remedy for concupiscence are proximate common goods which contribute splendidly to the production of the offspring according to the beautiful and orderly design of the Author of human nature. For these common goods are more readily obtained by the couple as they are a couple (conjugal society). But the development of this small society consisting of husband and wife gives rise to another more complex society (familial society) wherein friendship (love) and mutual aid have new meaning and superior quality. It is not for nothing that man is divided into male and female; without the two complementary members of the human species, the challenging task of reproducing ourselves could not be done with the same variety, the same efficiency (division of labor allows this), or the same excellence of offspring. For it would demand contradictory characters to be found in the same if we asked for one human being to do all that parents can do for their offspring. Nature does nothing in vain!

We are in the position to arrive at the conclusion now, from the principle governing ends in the practical order, that the reproduction of man depends on domestic society inasmuch as his *completion* demands that there be parental authority in educational matters. For this end, nature has marvelously provided the family wherein this authority is exercised. The parents, subjects of authority, have the obligation of completing what they have started and therefore to them belongs the right of educating their own child.

Argument II: From the Natural Inclination of Man to Marry and Have Children

This natural inclination was observed by Aristotle (and, we might add, the rest of mankind!) who proclaimed that man and woman "cannot exist without each other"[27] and they must enter into a union that "the race may continue."[28] He was much wiser than certain contemporaries who inform us that marriage is an invention of man, for Aristotle saw that the conjugal union comes from a "natural desire to leave behind them an image of themselves."[29] Such a design manifestly arises because nature has devised an instrument (the family) of reproducing the human race and has provided appropriate means towards that end. Messner makes the comment that, "education, which is the only thing that can develop this image in children, is therefore the task and privilege of the parents."[30] In other words, this natural inclination in the parents is the foundation of an obligation which in turn bestows on them the right to educate their own children, a moral power vis-a-vis all of mankind.

25

St. Thomas, commenting on the work of Aristotle, brings out the point that in all living things there is:

> [A] natural appetite to leave after themselves another of a similar nature to themselves, in such a way that through generation that might be preserved in the species which cannot be preserved in the numerically same individual.[31]

Hence, husband and wife can justly claim that "this thing is bigger than both of them" without tongue in cheek! For it is an urge founded in their nature and runs right throughout the whole of mankind.

St. Thomas, being the good metaphysician that he is, notes the continuity existing between parent and child whereby the former is reproduced in the very flesh of the latter:

> The father according to the flesh has in a particular way a share in that principle which in a manner universal is found in God...[32]

To steal the work of an artist is to steal not only the materials of which it is made but also the work, the artistry, and the love he has put into the production. How unjust it is to steal his beloved creation! He would regard the theft as a robbing of part of his being. In similar fashion, to take a child away from a parent is to steal his creation, his work of art, the object of his love, and the perfecting element to which so much time and productive effort has been given. Above all, the pride and joy of completing his projection of self is partly stolen. Such is the result of taking over the perfective aspect of rearing, that is, education, which would have the effect of denying the parental right to complete the natural impulse and inclination to have and develop one's own children.

Argument III: From the Natural Needs of the Child

If we consider the subject of the educative process, we are bound to arrive at the same conclusion concerning parental rights. For as Messner says:

> [N]ature speaks clearly for the parental function of education through the natural dependence of children on the parents and the resulting responsibility of the parents.[33]

This dependence is manifested in the following relationship with the parents:

A) A comparison with other animals manifests clearly that man takes a *much longer time* to attain maturity than any other member of the animal kingdom. Traditionally one attains manhood around the emancipative age of 21 years--allowing for variations according to the diverse civilizations and cultures--and up to this period education fulfills a role demanding great sacrifice motivated by love on the part of parents and child, much trial and error, failures, successes, but with progress in the development of the intellectual and moral virtues. All through this process, the existence of the child "clearly forms a part of the human existence of the parents."[34] He depends on them for the principles of his guidance, their application, and their correction in time of default. Such close supervision can only be given by parents in the early period, and later, still by the parents or others *supervised by the parents,* that is, those who stand in their stead.

John Locke, expressing the good common sense of the people, comments on the obligation of parents in terms of the needs of the child:

> The power...that parents have over their children arises from that duty which is incumbent on them, to take care of their offspring during the imperfect state of childhood. To inform the mind, and govern the actions of their yet ignorant nonage, till reason shall take its place and ease them of that trouble, is what the children want, and the parents are bound to.[35]

This "want" of children mentioned by Locke refers not to some capricious demand but rather to the demand of nature wherefrom all our properties spring.

B) Modern psychology has brought out the need of guidance and the part played by *hunger for security* in a child. Without the latter, harm could arrive in the life of the subject in several facets of his education whether it be emotive or intellective. One must note the urging of a parent robin as the youngsters prepare to leave the nest; consolation, recognition, and approval are needed more so in man because of his greater consciousness of self and awareness of the complexities of human existence. Above all, a child has a great *need of love* and wants to know that those who instruct him with authority, do so with love and, above all, love him for his own sake. Parents love their own child more than any other person can love him, loving him as part of themselves. Certain contemporary aberrations from this are, no doubt, due to the de-educative effect of television and other social influences which induce the *elicited* appetites (such as those drawn out by anger, frustration, etc.) sometimes masking *natural* appetites of love.

C) The child has, moreover, a natural *need of freedom* in keeping with his dignity as human. This freedom is more likely to arise from family influences than from political sources, and in keeping with the principle that, "a step towards dependence is a step away from independence, that is from freedom," we must avoid too much dependence on the state at all times

27

wherever possible. The greatest danger in socialistic education in which everyone is produced according to the same mold, is all too evident in the contemporary world. For higher authorities--and especially a government-- to assume the ultimate responsibility for educating a child, allows for dangerous developments within a political society which can only result in an eventual reduction of freedom.

Freedom is not desirable merely for its own sake, although that would be a sufficient reason; it is beneficial for the individual and the state inasmuch as the consequences within the body cultural, the body recreative, and the body economic as well as the body politic are immeasurable, given as much freedom as possible. Freedom is indeed truly a common good and hence, a condition of the good social well-being of any society.

D) Another natural need of a developing child, drastically overlooked by so many in our times, is the *safeguards* which exist in the family on account of its membership. Perhaps one of the most delicate matters is the gradual unfolding (maturation) of sexual knowledge in the mind of the developing child. He learns from the very warm and intimate association exhibited by both parents and other offspring. Association of images and concepts as well as the mention of small occurrences (one might think, for example, of the casual mention of "how long we had to wait for Betty to arrive"), not to speak of such obvious associations as the likeness between a son and his father and mother all come to mind. The son's daily contact with sisters allows for an awakening of consciousness and understanding, yet always with proper safeguards which protect both sisters and brothers--not the least of these being their consanguinity.

The intimacy of family life is by its very nature protective of the young and, at the same time, instructive, conditions which seem certainly overlooked by the protagonists of classroom sex education in current debates on this topic.

E) Yet a fifth need of the child is to be found in his requirement of *education for membership of civil society.* His first friends; his first opponents and indeed, enemies; those who first demand his allegiance; his first inquisitors; his first critics--those who first ridicule him; and yet, his first allies are all to be found within the security of the family circle. These experiences on a small scale, prepare him for the more profound experience which comes with membership of the larger social group. His mastership of himself, his prudential governance of his personal life, his need to apologize, his need to know who his friends really are, his need to learn to forgive, and his need to develop a true sense of values: these he learns within the family as a preparation for his political life as well as for the necessary conflicts, alliances, and negotiations with his fellow men.

F) A need which can be called "psychological," and which has received much attention in recent years, is the appetite for complete knowledge and certainty of *identity* in the mind of the offspring. Who the mother is, who the father is, what is his ancestry, what is his ethnic origin, what did his father do, the fad for establishing family trees, the boast that there is certain blood in the family (for example, Native American for Americans, convict ancestry for Australians, Norman French among French Canadians): the answer to these and many other questions satisfy the demand for knowledge of a whole cultural background as a stabilizing influence in the life of an offspring. But nothing short of a long apprenticeship at the feet of parents can satisfy all the questions which arise within the family circle on an ongoing basis. The parents alone can pass on this heritage as can be evidenced, to some extent, by the cultural continuity of the primitive peoples who pass on from generation to generation an often enormous tradition simply through constantly relating stories.

The length of time for the maturation process, the need for freedom with a feeling of security within family life, and yet, the existence of certain safeguards of the child so that he can spontaneously develop and conduct free inquiry among those immediately around him whom he can trust to speak and act with *his* best interest at heart: all of these concur as indicators that the parents are the true and certain supervisors of his education.

Argument IV: From the Principle of Subsidiarity

This well-known principle of reason can be accurately expressed as follows: "What can be done by the lower ought not be done by the higher."[36] For example, the manager of an enterprise ought not be a delivery clerk if there is another who can attend to that function. Likewise, the federal government ought not be responsible for tasks which can be the business of the states; county legislatures ought to attend to the affairs within their capacity while the state legislating bodies ought to leave well alone. Such a principle appears the more urgent as one recognizes the possibility of the absolute state.

The task of educating a child can be achieved within the domestic society and therefore ought to come directly under the jurisdiction of its parents. For the child as a person is a whole and has a personal end which belongs to him as an individual person. The guarantee of his *eternal* existence, which philosophers can demonstrate from utterly certain principles of reason, enables us to determine that the child is not merely a part of society and that the end of his existence is not merely the state itself, for he will still exist when the state has crumbled to dust or ashes. From this it clearly follows that education should perfect the individual for his own sake and not merely for the sake of the political society.

In the light of the principle of subsidiarity, it must be said that education should be provided by lower organizations and therefore lies beyond the function of the state. For the power of the latter enables the authorities to govern; that is their proper function. Hence, whatever lower body can

29

attend to education--especially the education of children--ought to attend to that task. Moreover, in view of the precious outcome which is essential to each individual person, civil society, and the human race, the more intimate the relationship, the better. The family is the only institution within the political society which can adequately meet these requirements.

It must not be forgotten that educatedness is a common good, but the process called education whereby we achieve that perfected state is a private good. This can be compared with *peace*, another common good. The state does not obtain peace but removes impediments to peace, which is obtained by the cooperative activity of the members of the community. Again, *order*, another common good, is obtained by the community acting cooperatively while the civil authorities, guardians of the common good, remove any citizen who becomes an impediment to that good. The common good is no less than the good of the body politic and at the same time, the good of each of its citizens.

There are goods which are private goods and yet at the same time, can be, in some manner, a common good. For example, *health* is a private good for it pertains to my health or your health. This is not the field of concern of the government. But at the same time, *public health* is the concern of the governing authority. For example, diseases being brought into the country from abroad, should be resisted or at least, its carriers removed from endangering the community. Hence, the need for quarantine.

In similar manner, the education of a child is a private good yet its *effect*, a well-informed citizenry with sufficient education rendering it more fit for societal existence, is the business of government. Any impediment to such development through education should be removed by the government. If, for instance, parents failed to educate a child, then their failure to meet their obligation should be pointed out to them and, if necessary, pressure brought to bear forcing them to meet their obligations. But the educational agency should not be the government any more than the agency to obtain peace and order in the community should be lawfully elected civil authority. This task falls on the shoulders of the people who in their daily activity produce those goods which we call "peace" and "order." The government, on the other hand, through its police force and civil courts, can remove whatever impedes the people from obtaining these common goods.

It should be noted that all the private goods do not add up to the public good. For example, all the private healths do not add up to the public health just as all the private monies of citizens do not add up to public monies. Similarly, all the private education, that is, the education of each of the private citizens, does not constitute a public good. The common good is an effect of the educative process, the latter being a precondition of the former. For a well informed public opinion, so necessary for a healthy political climate, results from a well educated people, each seeking his personal educatedness.

30

Men, women, and children all contribute to, and benefit from, the common good so that we can truly say that science, for example, is a social good as well as educatedness; the same can be said about art since it is a social good even though it resides in the intellects of individual persons. Indeed, we learn from and teach other on a daily basis as members of the community in which we live; we provide the opportunity for others to learn from us just as we learn from them.

In this notion of education properly understood is verified the true notion of a common good which can be accurately defined as "that good which is the good of the whole and the good of the parts." In other words, the common good of the United States is the good of the U.S.A. and the good of each American citizen.

The conclusion which follows from the above facts enlightened by the principle of subsidiarity can be stated as follows: The parents, belonging to the most basic social body (having the most basic or most particular function in the hierarchical structure of society), ought to be the functionaries responsible for the due education of their own offspring.

Argument V: From the Need for Unity (or Continuity) of the Educative Process

Implicit in this argument is the principle that there can be no coordination without subordination; in other words, without one responsible authority, that is, individual parents supervising these particular children, the education of the child would suffer. Cox notes the danger for all concerned if due attention were not given to this need for unity in the educative process:

> The task of parents cannot be usurped by others without destroying the unity of education, without perverting the natural and logical relation of domestic society to other societies and without imminent danger to human society. The nature of education demands in the first place that the educating principles should be vested with internal unity. This principle of internal unity would be destroyed, if others in their own right could inject themselves into the educative process.[37]

The obligation on parents to educate and to be in command, together with the unity necessary for ensuring the integrity of the educative process (i.e., a due organization of studies appropriate to that child), are all intimately associated. Redden and Ryan also note the disastrous effects on this unity should an attempt be made to remove parental authority:

> By the natural law, parents have the obligation

31

> of...educating their children. ...The family is the first
> agency destined by divine providence for this task,
> because if any other agency possessed an identical
> primary right, the unity of education would be
> destroyed.[38]

The unification of the educative process is seen by Messner from the viewpoint of the child and finds its source in the authority of the parents:

> Long before the growing child realizes himself as an
> individual and can understand the duty of obedience as
> a matter of conscience, he sees himself only as part of
> the family community and therefore wholly subject to
> the guidance and direction of the parents. Then, with
> the full development of reason this will be understood
> as the natural power of command which is based in
> the family community.[39]

Unity forms a natural element in the complex of security and in the confidence which springs from the love for, and knowledge of, the source of his existence with all of its dependences and ever-present personal resources. But, to attack the unity of some being is to attack its existence.[40] Hence, to take any action which might threaten the unity of the educative process will be to risk the development of the child. Therefore, we can legitimately conclude that one authority, the parents, being the closest and having all the benefits of consanguinity, should supervise the educative process and should not only have the obligation but should also have all consequent rights.

If the parents have the sole direct responsibility for the due education of their children, what can be said about the state's role in education, a phenomenon which has to be reckoned with in the contemporary world?

THE STATE AND EDUCATION (RECENT TRENDS)

One might legitimately ask if the state has the right to take over the education of the children-citizens of its families. But in order to answer such a question, we would do well to inquire into the nature of the authority which any state has; in other words, the question of the end for which civil society exists, must be determined.[41]

The Authority of the State

The function and authority of the state is evident from the good common sense of mankind as well as the judgment of various civil societies throughout the ages. For the highest task within any community is that of guarding the *common* good which is the *end* for which society exists.[42] Men and women are generally able to protect their *private* good but when it comes to the common good, that agency with the most common jurisdiction must be the guardian of the common good. Otherwise, there would be no higher functionary to attend to the supervisory task. In the meantime, since the principle of subsidiarity applies to any organization within the hierarchical structure, namely "what can be done by the lower ought not be done by the higher," any responsibility other than those pertaining to the common good ought to be left to lower functionaries.

Every government finds itself so preoccupied with an abundance of tasks, duties, and necessary fronts demanding attention, that if there is a way of avoiding direct involvement in some lesser responsibility, it ought to detach itself from such obligation. Is not a government sufficiently occupied with guarding civic friendship, peace, order, justice, freedom, ensuring that a healthy public opinion exists within the community and so on, without burdening itself with all the lower institutions of social order as if it were the task of the civil authority alone to supervise the attaining of their particular ends? This especially applies to the educational needs of the basic unit of the social group, namely, the family, since the parents are already available to attend to the complexities of family life.

Trend Toward Statism in General

The notable trend toward statism in the twentieth century as a reaction to the individualistic liberalism of the nineteenth century has been documented well enough.[43] From the utter freedom of the person alongside the denial of all social responsibility, to the utter dependence of man as a mere individual on civil society and its legally appointed authority, is but a short logical step.[44] Through the demand for a welfare society, men have moved to form a social group which gives protection to its citizens by robbing them of their dignity and self-governance (as individual persons).

The twentieth century has seen the rise of the totalitarian states in which nearly every phase of human existence has undergone a metamorphosis whereby the working man has changed one master for another. The unjust industrialist before whom he felt powerless has given way to a state authority. While the latter is bending over backwards to dispense justice, it crushes the working man, especially beneath the yoke of dependence--with its consequent loss of freedom--on the political organism which is encumbered by an enormous legal apparatus and bureaucracy.

Trend Toward Statism in Education

This move toward the absolute state has been no less noticeable in the field of education. Indeed, totalitarians have always been quick to seize the educational institutions as a means of controlling the citizenry.[45] They are quite aware that academic freedom poses a danger to their enterprise. The institutions of higher learning, especially, present a problem to the statist. Hence, the taking over of the schooling of young children becomes a supreme occupation as a prelude to controlling higher education. Once the indoctrination process has taken place, the semblance of academic freedom appears in the guise of a mature scholarship which has been truly deformed by earlier studies. Doesn't this appear to be happening in American universities, namely, one is free to teach according to one's best judgment and skill provided he does not go against the "party line," that is, the current relativism?

At the end of the nineteenth century, Herbert Spencer, in his *Principles of Ethics* commented on the tendency which in our day has become a crescendo:

> We have fallen upon evil times, in which it has come to be an accepted doctrine that part of the responsibilities are to be discharged not by the parents but by the public, a part which is gradually becoming a larger part and threatens to become the whole. Agitators and legislators have united in spreading a theory which, logically followed out, ends in the monstrous conclusion that it is for parents to beget children and for the state to take care of them. The political ethics now in fashion makes the unhesitating assumption that while each man, as parent, is not responsible for the mental culture of his offspring, he is, as a citizen, responsible for the mental culture of all other men's offspring! And this absurd doctrine has now become so well established that people raise their eyebrows in astonishment if you deny it. A self-evident falsehood has been transformed into a self-evident truth.[46]

The history of this tendency towards statism is based on a false notion of man, of the family and of the relationship of the child to the state together with an erroneous idea of the political organism. "The child belongs to the state" is a catchcry; "the good of the state depends on the good citizenry" is another; it is assumed that the unit of society is the individual person--and not the family. The attack on the family has arisen in modern times together with the denial of the eternal destiny of man and the affirmation of his supreme good as coinciding with the good of the state. This sets the tone for political atomism with each human person--children included--bearing a direct relation to the political group while denying any relation to the family and its organization. Thus children are not members of the conjugal unit but only members of civil society.

The claims of secular humanists--so active in our cultural milieu--give a further basis for this distorted thinking. One of their elite, H.J. Blackham, reveals his thinking in reply to the question, "Are humanists atheists or are they really agnostic?"; while informing us about secular humanism, he claims :

> As they assume that man is on his own and this life

> is all, humanists are virtually atheists, since practical
> decisions have to be made for the conduct of
> life...There is an essential combination of practical
> atheism with an agnostic temper in humanism...[47]

It follows logically from this teaching that the state alone exists as a person, existing for its own sake, alone having rights, and for which each man exists as a mere part. In other words man exists as an individual (a part) and not a person (a whole). It is assumed by the humanist that there is no afterlife and hence man has no eternal destiny. Thus his dignity as a person is denied. Does this not fittingly describe a dog or a tree? For they are mere parts of the species and exist for the good of the species and can be sacrificed for the good of the latter. Don't we sacrifice a bull calf if it ceases to have value for the herd; for example, if it fails to have the proportions appropriate for developing offspring either as good milkers or good beef producers?

Teachers steeped in the above error of secular humanism on such a basic point as the reason for man's whole existence, namely, to attain supreme perfection in a life to come, are hardly the desirable agents to minister to the educational needs of our children. That would be a consummate disaster!

It is but a short step from dependence on the state to acknowledging the state as the best proprietor of schools aimed at producing good citizens. This was the view taken by modern German educators and modern French politicians.[48] In the United States, educationists were not far behind the Europeans putting forward their claim for a state monopoly over educational establishments. Indeed, the socialism of schools has become so well established that parents sending their children to private schools are obliged to *subsidize* state school systems, an injustice which places a tremendous burden on the families of those conscientious enough to require a truly normal education for their children.

The attempt to produce an entirely socialized child, who will have *everything* in common with his fellows, has resulted in the acceptance of the local school board and its school system as the standard for schooling as if all other institutions were outside the realm of society, and merely to be tolerated.

We should note with some trepidation the remarks of one court in the United States:

> It is to be remembered that the public [that is, the
> State] *has a paramount interest in the virtue and
> knowledge of its members, and that, of strict right,
> the business of education belongs to it*...[P]arents are
> ordinarily entrusted with it...*but...what is there to
> prevent the public from withdrawing their faculties,
> held as they obviously are, at its sufferance?*[49]

35

In flat contradiction to the natural moral law, which is based upon the *nature* of man and the *nature* of civil society, courts have proclaimed that, "the authority of all guardians is derived from the [S]tate" and that "there is no parental authority independent of the supreme power of the [S]tate."[50] Further, the claim has been put forward that:

> [A] child is primarily a ward of the [S]tate. The sovereign [that is, the State] has the inherent power to legislate for its welfare, and to place [the child] with either parent at will, or take it from both parents and to place it elsewhere...the rights of the parent in his child are just such rights as the law gives him; no more, no less.[51]

The trend towards statism--or the absolute state--can also be seen in the utterances of certain educators as well as in the media. It is assumed that the state has an umbrella-like authority and the power to go far beyond its legitimate educational function mentioned above. This is seen in the multitude of state educational programs and agencies and state funding for them. Such funding is tacitly assumed to be a prime function of civil authority with, at the same time, a denial of justice to other educational institutions not set up by legislative bodies.

The local school board is "normal"; the function of political leaders is to help the people (a claim made without due distinction); these are the people's schools; it is a practical solution to education which follows from the will of the majority. Such defensive statements, when not offered openly, lie at the back of any public discussion of the problems being faced by the parents of a district. But these educational functions lie beyond the scope of governing the community!

The presumption of legitimacy of school taxes being paid to a local school while those who do not want to send their children to that school-- for reasons of conscience or other cause--are obliged to subsidize that civic program, has reached the point so that to claim otherwise is to arouse hostility. So-called "separation of church and state" is proposed as a principle whereby tax funds are denied private schools which are set up either at the request of parents or a parish. The parents are refused funding as if the local school board officially represented the state as a matter of justice.

If some families wish to contract with the state to set up a school district which will act in the place of the parents, they have that right, provided the parents retain control over their children's education, for example, the content. But to oblige others to pay taxes as a subsidy for that school-- parents who are unwilling and wish to arrange for a private means of education through some church or other organization--is contrary to the natural, moral law. For the power to mandate a district, publicly-organized school lies outside the powers related to the common good whereby is determined the function of a government.

Occasionally someone suggests a system of handouts or subsidies to return some of the taxes unjustly taken from parents who wish to choose their own system of schooling as if these grants were generous gifts of the government; but the latter should not have taken the taxes from the parents in the first place.

It is objected frequently that some parents do not know how to educate their children and therefore they have to give way to the authority of the state. But it is quite clear that the reason for mandating state education is not for the sake of quality but rather in order to gain control over it. For example, Adams and Stein, in their excellent work, *Who Owns the Children?*, relate the case of the Lippitts who, finding some of the material being taught to their children offensive, removed the latter from a state school and began teaching them at home. The Lippitts ultimately suffered jail sentences for their dedication, and a Cleveland newspaper, the *Plain Dealer*, commented on the event as follows:

> Any question of child abuse or neglect, at least as the terms are nominally understood, is patently absurd. The Lippitts obviously adore their children and, academically, as measured by the Standard Iowa Achievement Tests, they have done rather well by them; the children are ahead of the national average for their age groups.[52]

In the case of this beleaguered family, the quality of what was being taught was not questioned but rather it was evident that control was the end being sought. That the preservation of quality was not the motivation was made clear by the fact that the Lippitt girls in their educational development were "well ahead of the national averages for their age groups." Furthermore, it has been stated that this is not an isolated case but is now becoming the norm. Consider the famous case of the Gracey family, six of whose children were removed from their home by sheriff's officers because the parents refused to allow them to attend sex education classes at school.[53]

Grover, dealing with the many assaults which are being aimed at Christian educational organizations especially, and viewing the whole scene in general, states that:

> Not quality but conformity has been the criterion for judgment. The statutory purpose for the Minimum Standards--*quality*--is shunted aside in deference to [S]tate control.[54]

The intent to control the population could reach startling proportions. For instance, note what came from the Joint Commission on Mental Health of Children in a 1969 proposal:

> The child advocate, psychologist, social technician and medical technician should all reach *aggressively* into the community, send workers out to children's homes, recreational facilities and schools...*assume full responsibility for all education,* including pre-primary education, parent education and community education. Every child and youth in America *from conception* (nine months before birth) through age 24 are to be included.[55]

There seems little doubt that parental authority is being pushed aside in favor of absolute control by the state. Yet, this flies in the face of the conclusions reached by the U.S. Supreme Court when it was said that:

> It is cardinal with us that the custody, care and nurture of the child reside first in the parents, whose primary function and freedom include preparation for obligations the state can neither supply nor hinder.[56]

This judgment has been confirmed in another decision from which we learn that:

> The child is not the mere creature of the State; those who nurture him and direct his destiny have the right, coupled with the high duty to recognize and prepare him for additional obligations.[57]

Social philosophers and educators have with equal voice argued in favor of the rights of parents to be the educators of their children independently of the state. Leclercq, for example, notes the independence of the family from the state in its origins, for:

> [P]arents bring their children into the world on their own responsibility. At the same time they have the right and the duty to take care of them.
>
> They have the right because the family is an institution independent of the state. It springs spontaneously from man's very nature; the state does not have to create it.[58]

Rommen emphasizes the importance of the family notwithstanding the responsibility of the state even in the case of wayward parents:

> The family is prior to the state. The state may never

> take over entirely the end and functions of the family,
> even though it may have the duty, in virtue of its
> right of guardianship, to intervene in case this or that
> family is delinquent in its own duty.[59]

Messner argues from the lack of any juridical basis for the state to assume exclusive rights in education:

> There is no jural basis either for a state school
> monopoly or for compulsion to attend state schools.
> Parents have a natural right to found private schools
> if they wish and if their economic situation permits;
> in that case the state has merely the right to see that
> its standard of instruction is maintained. The state
> not only may not prevent the founding of private
> schools, but is even obliged by distributive justice to
> allot subsidies to these private schools out of the
> taxes, subsidies equal to the expenditure it saves
> through the private schools...If their educational
> rights are threatened by the state, the parents have a
> grave obligation to do everything in their power to
> reach a settlement of the schools question in harmony
> with their duties in the education of their children.[60]

If for some reason the legislative authority does have control of the educational system, as is the case in so many countries in the present era, then the autonomy of the parents ought to be recognized. Thornhill argues that any educational agency functions as an extension of parental right:

> The essential education of the child, in the sense of a
> guidance in the basic cultural orientation which is
> given to the child, belongs to the parents as a natural
> right. The work of specialized agencies is but an
> *extension* of what the parents have done, and the
> supervision of it belongs to the parents as the
> extension of their right. The principle of social
> autonomy assigns this prerogative to them, and the
> educational agencies...are responsible to the parents in
> the carrying out of their task.[61]

The State Has No Direct Rights in Education

Just as arguments can be proposed to defend the natural jurisdiction of parents over the education of their children, so arguments exist to demonstrate that the state does not have direct and exclusive rights over that domestic function. In other words, it is shown in these arguments that it is not the proper domain of the political authority although it does follow that the latter has indirect rights. The principles from which we argue are those very same principles whereby it is shown in political ethics that all forms of socialism are contrary to the natural order of the civil society. Some of the arguments in summary form are as follows:

Argument I: From the End of Civil Society [62]

The natural end of the political group, as is the case with any social group, is the common good. Some of the more principal of these goods can be stated as follows: civic friendship, peace and order, justice and freedom. But it is the function of the government to be guardian of the common good, that is, its proper function is to govern the people so that they will all coordinate toward the common good, that is, the goods which are common to each member of civil society and to the civil society itself.

On the other hand, the ends of lesser social groups do not come within the ambit of the common good of the totality, that is to say, the common good of lesser bodies (for example, sporting clubs, cultural organizations) is obtained by a particular group and not by the civic group (thus each lower group requires its own governing agency).

Therefore, it belongs to the parents to have the responsibility of governing the education of their own children. Therefore, it does not belong to the government to govern directly the education of children.

Argument II: From the Principle of Subsidiarity [63]

As stated earlier in this essay, this principle expresses the natural dictate that jurisdiction over lesson moral bodies should be delegated to lower functionaries. Therefore, since the work of supervising education *can* be done by lower bodies (i.e., the domestic society), it is not the function of civil society to take responsibility for the education of children.

Argument III: From the Common Good Which is Freedom

From the principle which states that "a step towards dependence is a step away from independence," it can be shown that any move toward dependence on the government takes us away from independence; this loss of independence is nothing less than a loss of freedom. On the other hand, we have seen above that one of the basic needs of a child is freedom. This need is the more serious as we realize that it is necessary for the full development of the child in its growth towards maturity. The acquisition of prudence alone demands this. Therefore, every citizen, children included, ought to have independence from government control wherever possible. Aristotle warned us twenty-four centuries ago, but we are still not listening. For he concluded that there can be too much unity in a state. In reply to the remark of Socrates that "'the greater the unity of the state the better,'" Aristotle objected:

> Is it not obvious that a state may at length attain
> such a degree of unity as to be no longer a state?...we

40

> ought not attain this greatest unity even if we could,
> for it would be the destruction of the state.[64]

The philosopher goes on to note the danger inherent in the designs of planners who would force a simplistic unity on our political structure, explaining that, "[T]here is a point at which a state may attain such a degree of unity as to be no longer a state, or at which, without actually ceasing to exist, *it will become an inferior state.*" [65]

It would not be difficult to foresee the outcome of extreme unity within the social organism; it would cease to be as an organism. The organicity consists in parts adapted to special functions, each with its particular interest expertly providing goods, services, recreative and cultural undertakings for the community. The free operation of so much expertise would be lost!

The greatest loss of freedom is in the intellectual order. The denial of educational liberty is a cultural disaster. In consequence, it is difficult to correct all other kinds of error, injustice, and impediments to human happiness.

Conclusion

We should heed the warning of Messner about the folly of yielding all parental rights in education to the state. He tells us that even J.S. Mill, a leading figure in modern liberalism, emphasized the fact that a state school monopoly would both endanger parental rights and liberty and harm the good of society and the advancement of civilization. Mill says that while the state may rightfully require that everyone gain certain knowledge, it has no authority to mandate how and from whom it is to be acquired. Messner observes that modern totalitarian states have shown that a government can use a state school monopoly to shape the young in whatever way it wishes.[66]

If we allow the state this supposed civil right, we have nothing to lose, only our freedom--and perhaps much more!

THE URSURPATION OF PARENTAL VALUES

The trend toward replacing parents with state agencies is bad enough but what constitutes education in the minds of some educators is most revealing and exacerbates any tendency to state control. For some have no hesitation in declaring that the whole moral formation of children will be determined according to certain ideological presuppositions in conflict with traditional ideals; the prognosis can be termed at least "ominous." For example, they see the schools as agents for changing the whole moral fiber of our society thrusting aside all established values, notwithstanding their basis in the natural moral law.

41

Nesbitt informs us that Dr. John Goodlad, an educationist, in a report to the President's Commission on School Finance, supported this notion:

> [T]he majority of our youth still hold the values of their parents and if we do not alter this pattern, if we do not resocialize ourselves to accept change, our society may decay.[67]

But one might well wonder why our society will decay if we do not resocialize ourselves. Moreover, what is wrong with the values of our parents? Are we not merely assuming that a certain ideological position, in opposition to traditional values, is a valid position?

Another comment, this time by Paul Brandwein, is also enlightening. He claims that, "Any child who believes in God is mentally ill."[68]   It might be noted in passing that the evidence for the existence of God, so clearly presented by some philosophers, is not attacked but there is merely an *ad hominem* (personal) remark made concerning the mental competence of children. Ashley Montagu reinforces this adverse judgment concerning the condition of our offspring with his claim that "The American family structure produces mentally ill children."[69]

The contempt for the authority of those responsible for the education of our youth, the parents, is quite evident, but there is much more in the educational ideologists' arsenal of destructive thinking. From Dr. Pearce of Harvard University, we have the following revealing statement:

> Every child in America who enters school at the age of five is mentally ill, because he comes to school with allegiance toward our elected officials, toward our founding fathers, toward institutions, toward the preservation of this form of government w e have...patriotism, nationalism, sovereignty...All of that proves the children are sick, because the truly well individual is one who has rejected all of those things and is what I would call the true international child of the future.[70]

Small wonder that we have seen traitorous behavior from some Americans within our midst during recent years if such an attitude is being fostered by our educational system!

This rather dubious estimation of American children, which in reality pronounces upon the competence of parents to rear their own offspring, is echoed by the National Training Laboratories, conducted by the National Education Association, in presenting its position (which is akin to that of a totalitarian dictator):

> Although [children] appear to behave appropriately
> and seem normal by most cultural standards, they
> may actually be in need of mental health care, in order
> to help them change, adapt and conform to the
> planned society in which *there will be no conflict of
> attitudes or beliefs.*[71]

This advocating of psychologically coercive methods on healthy children, claimed to be mentally ill, for the purposes of controlling and adapting all thinking to conform with the ideological ambitions of certain educators, manifests just how far some are prepared to go in determining the future of a nation; the education responsibilities of parents will not be allowed to stand in the way. The latter will be replaced by the ideologues who assume a certain competence while making judgments in conformity with standards based upon the doctrinal position of movements or groups endowed with the secular humanist ideology and popularized situationist ethics.[72]

While the usurpation of parental rights has been flagrantly carried out with a dignified authoritativeness on the academic and political level, a more openly adversary attitude has been adopted at the so-called "grassroots." Educationists and teachers, disregarding parents, have often carried on a deception of those who confidently send their children to schools where they are being indoctrinated in new courses reaching far into the private domain of the family. As an illustration, it is fruitful to examine some of the statements made by educators in recent years. Nesbitt, relates, for example, that Sidney Simon has informed us that teachers have had "major success by closing their doors and doing things they believe in."[73] But further remarks from Simon, when he was teaching at Temple University, assure us of his intent:

> I always bootlegged the *values stuff* under other titles.
> I was assigned to teach Social Studies in the
> Elementary School and I taught values clarification. I
> was assigned Current Trends in American Education
> and I taught my trend.[74]

As if this deception is not enough, we are given an inkling elsewhere of the kind of objectives Simon had in mind as he describes the activities of some educators behind closed doors. They operate as "change agents," a term which has been defined as signifying "a person, organization or institution that changes or helps to change the beliefs, values, attitudes or behavior of people *without their knowledge or consent.*"[75]

Simon also informs us that, "When the teacher closes the classroom door in the morning and is alone with the students, the real curriculum begins."[76]

43

It is clear that the values of parents will be superseded in the planning and operations of these educators.

On the other hand, many of us have been witness to the reports of humiliation suffered by some parents who, while endeavoring to ascertain more accurately the content of courses being offered in such personal matters as sex education and so-called "parenting" courses,[77] have been insulted and verbally abused, even being declared "trouble-makers." Having spoken before certain educational bodies and witnessed the disinterest and even hostility to parental requests for a hearing, I am sensitive to the anguish of families in their efforts to ensure that their small charges are not being intellectually and emotionally seduced. The subtle indoctrination by means of questionnaires, scenes being acted out (suicide included), and moral dilemmas[78] being put before immature minds certainly not equipped to see through the propaganda being imposed on them, escapes many parents and even teachers, in my experience.

The teacher of ethics finds some of the ethical problems being submitted to young minds perplexing enough; hence, those young people lacking maturity and the principles and method of a difficult science--the science of ethics--must fall foul of the many snares lying in wait for the amateur. What a glorious opportunity to persuade the next generation that we should bring in suicide, abortion, euthanasia, and perhaps genocide, while at the same time, accepting abnormal moral states (such as homosexuality), not to mention establishing a one-world government! Thus would be satisfied the ideological and political ambitions of those who would thrust on mankind a spurious unity so strongly condemned by Aristotle.

The statements of certain activists interested in education recorded above should be sufficient to warn us that there are some whose values set the good of the individual child far below that of the public good. They would be prepared to sacrifice the private good for the sake of the public good. With an achievement such as this, we would be assured of harming the latter in the long run.

No educator can afford to lose sight of the responsibility he shoulders for his charges--his students--on account of the proven immortality of the human soul, which will continue to exist long after their country has crumbled to dust and ashes. For theirs is an eternal destiny!

On the other hand, even temporal happiness demands that human nature develop into the fulness of the perfection which is consonant with that nature adequately understood. Parents have a connatural knowledge of their own child and an instinctive apprehension of the care, supervision, and correction needed to aid that true evolution. They will not be deceivers of their own children; they will, moreover, prefer the good of the offspring for the sake of the latter. Children need to be educated, for example, for their own sake quite unlike any other living organism. That is the best way to produce good citizens!

TRUE PHILOSOPHY OF EDUCATION

The education of a child can make or break him; as a result, the nation either benefits or is broken with its children. That flows from the principle enunciated by Aristotle when he warned us that:

> The *least initial* deviation from the truth is multiplied later a thousandfold....The reason is that a principle is great rather in power than in extent; hence that which was small at the start turns out a giant in the end.[79]

The same philosopher emphasized this again elsewhere:

> [P]rinciples, though small in size, are great in potency; this, indeed, is what is meant by a principle, that it is itself the cause of many things without anything else being higher than it is for it to depend upon.[80]

What is the meaning of this warning? First of all, we are being told that fundamental principles in any order can lead either to great error or to a true edifice of artistic or scientific truth. Hence, to deviate from sound principles or to assume the truth of erroneous principles in matters of *education* can only lead to a disastrous situation for the child and the civil society in which he lives. The basis of his learning having been warped, there cannot but be a very poor sense of values and consequently, chaos in the practical order. For the errors in principle will be magnified in the many conclusions to be drawn in the sciences and the arts. In our daily life, both personal and social, the practical outcome must be unhappiness. Are we not, for example, all familiar with the consequences of false political principles where the errors lead to discontent and a destruction of peace and order? In fact, the first place this can be seen is in the body economic. But, the danger acruing from false educational principles is far more serious as we saw above.

On the other hand, adhering to true fundamental principles is indispensable for a true educational development. This in its turn, with the knowing powers correctly informed, will lead to the unfolding of man's capacities for virtue and understanding with a consequent liberation (hence, the liberal arts) from enslavement to lower things and human passion. For a true sense of values brings harmony to the human soul and consequently, to the whole psychophysical organism. The benefits to each child and to human society, if left to themselves, will inevitably be multiplied. Hence, if we are to avoid the many pitfalls in the education of a child, we ought first understand what the nature of education is.

In keeping with this that the end is principle in the practical order, all education ought to be tailored towards the *supreme end* for which man exists; in other words, the ultimate purpose of his existence brings into being all other designs, organizations, and operations within man's life. It is indeed as the ancients expressed it: "The cause of causes." Moreover, education ought to bring awareness of the totality of human life and its journey towards that indisputably evident goal of all of our struggles.

To be truly educated is manifestly a condition whereby man is able not only to live but to live well, and that includes living among his fellow-men; in other words, to conduct himself happily and fruitfully in the political society. Hence, education is a necessary preparation for social well-being in the company of men.

Christian education and sound, scientifically developed philosophy go further, demanding that man be prepared for, in addition to the natural order, his supernatural end, that is, for the life after the present earthly dwelling. Hence, it is imperative that the *end* for which man exists determine the nature of true education.

Every child born becomes a member of at least three societies: the family, the political group, and the Christian society (when and if he is baptized).[81] He might reject one or the other but he cannot escape the demand of his nature for the perfections derived from these three social groups. Just as a lawfully appointed authority is needed within the political organism to conform to the principle that "there can be no coordination without subordination," so likewise there is needed in the education of a child some subordinating authority to ensure that there will be coordination towards the final cause.

Parents, with their special love for their own offspring, are irreplaceable as the overseers of the developing child; they will have in sight at all times the necessary and due perfection being sought as a preparation for that ultimate end.

It goes without saying that not only parents but civil authorities ought to have some knowledge of the nature and principles of true education so that the well-being of both the child and of civil society might be maintained. The latter might suffer considerably if the needs of the new live man cannot be satisfied so that he might survive and develop as he ought, "to the perfection of man considered as man, that is, to a state of virtue"[82] as advised by St. Thomas.

Man is endowed with a number of powers of operation, his faculties. But these should be perfected by virtues (or qualities) so that they can function with all the fulness of their operation and permit man to be master of his destiny. Knowledge of his own nature, including his vegetative and sensitive powers as well as his rational powers is of great advantage to every man and woman. This is necessary to help us overcome the weaknesses of human nature, notably, the darkness of the intellect, the weakness of the will, and eruption of the pleasurable and aggressive passions which are always straining at the leash.

In other words, development or maturation consists in the production of *qualities* in the operative powers of the human soul; that is, the faculties of the soul have added to them perfecting qualities or forms enabling the soul's powers to operate with facility and indeed, giving us the power to function intellectually and morally with greater ease. These qualities are called "virtues" (Latin: *vis* = force or power → *vir* or man → *virtus* or virtue). The qualities are led out from the capacity of the soul's powers, hence we speak of the process whereby they are developed as "education" (Latin: *e+ ducere*: to lead out from) and the result as "educatedness," a term usually confused with the term "education," but which properly signifies the effect of education.

Two kinds of virtues require to be developed: intellective virtues (allowing us to *understand* well both in the speculative order and the practical order); and the moral virtues (helping us to *act* well and wisely in all of our *free* human actions)[83] :

A) *The intellectual virtues* can be detailed as follows:
    1) Virtues in the intellect performing its *speculative* operations (knowing for the sake of knowing):
        a) Understanding (Intelligence): Knowledge of basic principles of reason.
        b) Science: Certain knowledge through causes.
        c) Wisdom: Certain knowledge through *ultimate* causes.
    2) Virtues in the intellect performing its *practical* operations (practical intellect) (knowing for the sake of doing):
        a) Synderesis: Knowledge of basic practical principles of reason.
        b) Prudence: Right reason about things to be done (knowing how to act correctly *here and now*.)
        c) Art: Right reason about things to be made.

B) The second element of education is the development of *the moral virtues* which perfect our human *actions*. These are the following together with the power they perfect:

Virtue   *Power*

Prudence perfecting the Intellect
Justice perfecting the Will
Temperance perfecting the Pleasurable appetites (Concupiscible)
Fortitude perfecting the Aggressive appetites (Irascible)

These virtues "empower" us to *act* well and with control; for example,

47

justice with respect to the rights of others; temperance with respect to pleasurable things, giving us true control; fortitude with respect to difficult things, again giving us true control; finally, prudence, which helps us to determine how to apply the other virtues *here and now*, that is, in these circumstances and on this occasion. The latter, prudence, is the key to the formation of a good virtuous life through the employment of good judgment, the effect of prudence.

It will also be observed that prudence is among the intellective (intellectual) *and* moral virtues; this to be expected, for the intellect in its application of practical principles (synderesis) requires the guidance granted by prudence so that those principles can be applied here and now in situations where pleasurable and difficult matters have to be considered. Prudence helps us to arrive at a more certain conclusion of what action ought to be taken in *these* circumstances since motives and circumstances can pose serious dilemmas. Virtue is not mere *knowledge* as some of the ancients thought; hence prudence is not the only virtue. Moreover, practice is required to acquire not only prudence but the other three virtues as well in order to be able to respond well when faced with the right circumstances.

Since the development of the child is a most intimate affair, demanding of the parents constant sacrifice, constant supervision, and constant correction, and therefore constant love--the moving power which drives a parent to make the necessary sacrifices--it is clear that the parents alone fill the role of true education. Theirs alone can be the task of supervising *what* education is given to the child as well as *who* gives it. For they alone are equipped with the connatural knowledge of that particular child; for the child is the extension of the personality of the parents.

CONCLUSION

The state at its own peril will interfere with family life by way of assuming full control of the education of children, either by taking total control of finances, or, assuming sole proprietorship of the instruments of education (such as buildings)--and all without the consent of parents. Such absolute jurisdiction over the educative process lies beyond the authority derived from the natural moral law for those who have been duly elected to govern civil society. Whatsoever administrative activity lies outside the common good--measure of government authority--ought to be left to those who have given birth to the ones to be educated. Indeed, the United States Supreme Court in a decision on an important controversy declared that:

> The fundamental theory of liberty upon which all governments in this Union repose excludes any general power of the State to standardize its children by forcing them to accept instruction from public teachers only.[84]

If the educational system develops in a direction which runs counter to the best interest of its future citizens, and especially its youngest members of society not yet intellectually, emotionally, and morally formed, then there would be no safeguard to protect the body cultural.

A truly human system of education should take into account the subject of the process, namely, the child. For the enormous varieties in temperaments, interests, and capacities for the life of the mind demand free reign so that individual preferences for the vast array of studies available to man might find their best outlet and proper development. Otherwise, if the government had direct control of the education of children, this would be an excellent case of that extreme unity rejected by Aristotle, for "extreme unification of the state is clearly not good."[85] This will be even more apparent when that unity runs into conflict with freedom of the will being exercised in the body cultural--especially in matters of education.

NOTES

1. Cf. Krason, Stephen M. & D'Agostino, Robert J., eds., *Parental Rights: The Contemporary Assault on Traditional Liberties.* (Front Royal, Va: Christendom College Press), 1989, *passim.*

2. *Ibid.*; McGraw, Onalee, *The Family, Feminism, and the Therapeutic State.* (Wash., D.C.: Heritage Fdn., 1980), *passim*; Adams, Blair & Stein, Joel, *Who Owns the Children?* Education as Religious War, Bk. Five (2nd ed.; Grand Junction, Colo., 1984), *passim*

3. Aristotle, *Nicomachean Ethics*, VIII, c. 12, 1161b, 28-35. The quotes from and references to Aristotle's writings were taken from different editions : *Aristotle's Ethics* , ed. & trans. John Warrington (N.Y.: Dutton [Everyman's Library], 1963); *The Basic Works of Aristotle* , ed. Richard McKean (N.Y.: Random House, 1941); and *The Politics* , trans. Bejamin Jowett (N.Y.: Modern Library, 1943).

4. *Ibid.*, VIII, c. 12, 1161b, 24-25; cf. Locke, John, *Second Essay Concerning Civil Government,* Chap. VI, n. 67 Hutchins, Robert Maynard, ed. in chief, *Great Books of the Western World.* (Chicago: Encyclopedia Brittanica, Inc., 1952; Vol. 35, "Locke, Berkeley, Hume."); cf. Leclercq, Jacques, *Marriage and the Family,* trans. Thomas R. Hanley (Rev. ed.; N.Y.: Frederick Pastet, 1942), p. 9 *et seq.*

5. Thomas Aquinas, *Summa Theologica*, 3 vols., trans. Fathers of the English Dominican Province (N.Y.: Benzinger Bros., 1947), Suppl., q. 41, a.1.

6. Leclereq, Chap. 1. In *The Politics,* II, cc. 3 and 4, Aristotle criticizes Plato for his suggestion concerning the community of wives; cf. the concern shown by Aristotle for the due education of children in Aristotle's *Politics* VII, c. 17. The teaching of the latter contrasts sharply with the reports contained in a work edited by Phyllis Schlafly, *Child Abuse in the Classroom* (Alton, Ill.: Pere Marquette Press, 1984), which contains "excerpts from Official Transcript of Proceedings" of hearings before the U.S. Department of Education in the Matter of Proposed Regulations to Implement the

Protection of Pupil Rights Amendment, Sec. 439 of the GEPA (the "Hatch Amendment").

7. Redden, John D. & Ryan, Francis A., *A Catholic Philosophy of Education.* (Milwaukee: Bruce, 1942), p. 108.

8. Thomas Aquinas, *Summa Contra Gentiles* (Trans. into English under the title of: *On the Truth of the Catholic Faith;* Garden City, N.Y.: Doubleday, 1955-56, 5 vols.), III, c. 112; Thomas Aquinas, *Summa Theologica,* II-II, q. 64, a.5, reply obj. 3.

9. Thomas Aquinas, *On the Truth...,* II, q. 11, a.1, and ad 4, 7, 9, 11.

10. Aristotle, *Nicomachean Ethics,* VIII, c. 12, 1162a, 16-30, cf. Thomas Aquinas, *Summa Theologica,* I, q. 6, a. 1.

11. Cf. Janssens, Ed., *Les droits due pere de famille en matiere* d'education et d'enseignement (Liege, 1930), p. 12, cited in Leclereq, p . 351.

12. Cf. Thomas Aquinas, *Summa Contra Gentiles,* III, c. 81; Thomas Aquinas, *Summa Theologica,* II-II, q. 64, aa. 2,3; Leclercq, pp. 350-358.

13. Cf. Locke, Chap. VI, n. 67.

14. Cf. Dionisius the Areopagite, *On the Divine Names and the Mystical Theology,* C.E. Rolt, ed. (London, 1920), cap 4, n. 20 (pp. 3, 720); cf. Thomas Aquinas, *Summa Theologica,* I, q. 5, a. 4, ad 2.

15. Aristotle, *DeAnima,* II, c. 4, 415a, 23-415b, 8.

16. Pope Pius XI, *Christian Education of Youth,* section on "Family."

17. Thomas Aquinas, *Summa Theologica,* II-II, q. 102, a. 1.

18. *Ibid.,* II-II, q. 10, a. 12.

19. The pleasurable appetites or passions are: love and hatred; desire and aversion; joy and sadness. The aggressive appetites or passions are: hope and despair; boldness and fear; and anger. (Cf. Thomas Aquinas, *Summa Theologica,* I, qq. 80-81; Thomas Aquinas, *Ont he Truth...,* q. 25, a. 2; Aristotle, *Nicomachean Ethics,* VII, cc. 6-7.

20. Aristotle, *Politics,* I, c. 2, 1252b, 31-1253a, 1.

21. Aristotle, *Nicomachean Ethics,* VII, c. 8, 1151a, 16.

22. Thomas Aquinas, *Summa Theologica,* I-II, q. 90, a.1.

23. Thomas Aquinas, *Commentary on Aristotle's Physics,* II, lect. 15, n. 273.

24. Thomas Aquinas, *Summa Theologica,* Suppl., q. 41, a.1.

25. Redden & Ryan, pp. 107-110.

26. Aristotle, *Nicomachean Ethics,* VIII, c.12, 1162a, 16-19.

27. Aristotle, *Politics*, I, c.2, 1252a, 27.

28. *Ibid.*, 28.

29. *Ibid.*, 30-31.

30. Messner, Johannes, *Social Ethics: Natural Law in the Western World,* trans. J.J. Doherty (Rev. ed.; St. Louis: B. Herder, 1965), p. 410.

31. Thomas Aquinas, *In I Politic.*, c. 1, n. 18; cf. note 11; cf. note 11, *supra.*

32. Thomas Aquinas, *Summa Theological,* II-II, q. 102, a.1.

33. Messner, p. 410.

34. *Ibid.*

35. Locke, Chap. VI, n. 58.

36. Cf. Messner, pp. 209-217.

37. Cox, Ignatius W., *Liberty, Its Use and Abuse* (3rd ed.; N.Y.: Fordham University Press, 1946), p. 333.

38. Redden & Ryan, p. 108.

39. Messner, p. 411.

40. Thomas Aquinas, *Summa Theologica,* I, q. 11, a.1, c.; cf. n. 12 above.

41. See note 11 above.

42. Cox, pp. 370-376; Thornhill, John, *The Person and the Group.* (Milwaukee: Bruce, 1967), Chap. 9, note especially p. 159; cf. Messner, pp. 579-582.

43. Gonsalves, Milton A., *Fagothey's Right and Reason* (9th ed.; Columbus, Ohio: Merrill, 1989); Roesch, Eugene J., *The Totalitarian Threat* (N.Y.: Philosophical Library, 1963); Neill, Thomas P., *1859 in Review* (Westminister, Md.: Newman, 1959); Catherine, Victor, *Socialism: Its Theoretical Basis and Practical Application* (8th ed., rev.; N.Y.: Benzinger Bros., 1904), p. 224 *et seq.*; Maritain, Jacques, *The Person and the Common Good* , trans. John J. Fitzgerald (N.Y.: Chas. Scribner's Sons, 1947), Chap. V.

44. *Ibid.*; cf. Belloc, Hilaire, *The Servile State.* (London: Constable, 1927).

45. Cf. Krason & D'Agostino, *passim;* cf. Hitler, Adolph, e.g. in *Philosophy: Readings from Plato to Gandhi* (Garden City, N.Y.: Doubleday [Anchor], 1963), pp. 460-462 (selections from *Mein Kampf* dealing with education in Hitler's Germany); cf. Rommen, Heinrich, *The State in Catholic Thought: A Treatise in Political Philosophy* (St. Louis: B. Herder, 1950), Chap. XV, Sect. 1.

46. Spencer, Herbert, *Principles of Ethics*, cited in Cox, p. 328.

51

47. Blackham, H.J., *Humanism* (Harmondsworth: Penguin Bks. Ltd. [Pelican Original], c. 1968), p. 190.

48. Waters, Raphael T., "The Basis for the Traditional Rights and Responsibilities of Parents," Krason & D'Agostino, pp. 13-18.

49. *Ex parte Walters*, 221 P.2d 659, 667 (Okla., 1908), cited in Adams & Stein, p. 40, [emphasis in the original].

50. *Allison v. Bryan*, 97 P. 282, 287, (Okla., 1908), quoting *Mercein v. People*, 25 Wend. (N.Y.) 99, cited in Adams & Stein, p. 40.

51. *Allison v. Bryan*, 97 P. 282, 286; cited in *ibid.*

52. Grover, Alan N., "The Day the State Took Amy and Alice," *CLA Defender* (June 1978), p. 18, cited in Adams & Stein, p. 16.

53. Likoudis, James, "Classroom Sex Education: Undermining Parental Rights," Krason & D'Agostino, p. 109.

54. Grover, Alan N., "Ohio's Trojan Horse," p. 6, cited in Adams & Stein, p. 17 (emphasis added). It is interesting to note the increasing number of complaints concerning schooling being received by the Christian Law Association, as reported by Adams & Stein, (emphasis added).

55. Lowrie, Reginald, President, Joint Commission on Mental Health of Children, Report to U.S. Congress, as cited in Nesbitt, Vince, *Humanistic Morals and Values Education* (Lane Cove, New South Wales, Australia: V. Nesbitt, 1981), p. 6, (emphasis added).

56. *Prince v. Massachusetts*, 321 U.S. 158, 166 (1944).

57. *Pierce v. Society of Sisters*, 268 U.S. 510, 535 (1925).

58. Leclercq, p. 351.

59. Rommen, Heinrich, *The Natural Law*, trans. Thomas R. Hanley (St. Louis: B. Herder, 1947), pp. 238-239; cf. Laclercq, pp. 358 ff.

60. Messner, p. 656.

61. Thornhill, p. 207, (emphasis is his).

62. Thomas Aquinas, *On Kingship, The Political Ideas of St. Thomas Aquinas*, ed. Dino Bigongiari (N.Y.: Hafner, 1969), Chap. 1, nn. 3, 8-10; Maritain, Chap. IV.

63. Messner, pp. 209-217, 630-634.

64. Aristotle, *Politics*, II, c. 2, 1261a, 16-17, 23-24.

65. *Ibid.*, c. 5, 1263b, 33-35; cf. 1261b, 9, (emphasis added).

66. Messner, p. 657.

67. Goodlad, John, *Schooling for the Future. A Report to the President's Commission on School Finance*, Issue No. 9, Report of Task Force C (Los Angeles): Education Inquiry, Inc., 1971) p. 14, cited in Nesbitt, p. 4.

68. Brandwein, Paul, *The Social Sciences* (N.Y.: Harcourt, Brace, Jovanovich, 1970), cited in Nesbitt, p.5.

69. Ashley Montagu in a lecture at Anaheim, Calif. before 1,000 home economics teachers, Nov. 1970, cited in Nesbitt, p.5.

70. Dr. Pierce in an address to teachers in Denver, Colo., in 1973, cited in "Education to Remold the Child," *Parent and Child Advocate*, Watertown, Wis., p. 30, which is cited in Nesbitt, p.5.

71. National Training Laboratories, *Issues in Training*, p. 47, cited in Nesbitt, p. 5, (emphasis added).

72. Cf. Nesbitt, *passim.*

73. Gray, Farnum, "Doing Something About Values," *Learning* (1972), cited in Nesbitt, p. 14.

74. *Ibid.* (Emphasis added).

75. Morris, Barbara M., *Change Agents in the Schools* (Ellicott City, Md., 1979), p. 15, cited in Nesbitt, p. 6, (emphasis added).

76. Alexander, William M., *Changing the Curriculum Content* (Wash., D.C.: Association for Supervision and Curriculum Development, 1964), p. 13, cited in Nesbitt, p. 14.

77. Schlafly, ed., pp. 31, 52, 102-103, 206, 248.

78. *Ibid., passim.*

79. Aristotle, *On the Heavens*, I, c. 5, 271b, 10-13, (emphasis added).

80. Aristotle, *On the Generation of Animals*, V, 788, 12.

81. Cf. Pope Pius XI, *Christian Education of Youth, ad init*; Conway, Pierre, *Principles of Education. A Thomistic Approach* (Wash., D.C.: The Thomist Press, 1960), Chap. 1.

82. Thomas Aquinas, *Summa Theologica*, Suppl., q. 41, a. 1.

83. Conway, pp. 11-12; Gonsalves, pp. 204-210; Aristotle, *Nicomachean Ethics*, Bk. VI; Thomas Aquinas, *Summa Theologica*, I-II, q. 57.

84. *Pierce v. Society of Sisters, supra*, at 535.

85. Aristotle, *Politics*, II, c. 2, 1261b, 11.

THE PURPOSE OF LIBERAL EDUCATION

by J. Donald Monan, S.J.

It has been more than two decades since Daniel Bell wrote his landmark summary of *The Recent History of Liberal Arts Education in America*, and provided what he hoped would be a blueprint to revitalize the liberally educative mission of undergraduate colleges and universities. His historical reading of the lofty intentions and ambitions of curricula that had characterized the University of Chicago, Columbia, and Harvard, found each of those programs when he wrote in 1966, in the words of one reviewer, to be "reduced to a junkyard of unrelated fragments."

Many of the pressures that weakened the vitality of liberal education in our institutions we are all familiar with, and they have been reflected upon in studies again more recently: pressures upward, from a growingly professionalized and differentiated society in which specialized skills are a condition of entrance and mobility; and within the undergraduate colleges themselves, the increasing specialization and departmentalization and consequent isolation of faculty members and their offerings. Under the centrifugal pressure of departmental specializations, coherence and unity in programs of liberal education broke down, and perhaps the best that remained, as has again recently been said, was a distribution requirement to guarantee at least a certain breadth to a young person's education as the counterweight to increasing depth of his or her specialization.

My purpose, however, is to say that there are two other reasons, more fundamental still, for the present aimlessne; s and lack of coherence in programs of liberal education. These forces, if addressed, would allow for

55

the reintegration of departmental specializations and the differentiated competences that will remain a necessity of our modern world, and certainly of citizenship. But if unaddressed, they will continue to frustrate every measure of ingenuity and artfulness employed to resolve our current impasses.

Stated simply, most colleges and universities, in my view, attempt the reconstruction of their liberal education programs from the raw materials of intellectual disciplines themselves that are represented among their faculties. And so immediately the question arises as to whether mathematics is not as potent a mind trainer as German, whether on intellectual merit one social science is not just as valuable as another in the training of the liberally educated person. It is my belief that colleges should start not with the raw materials of intellectual disciplines, but with as clear and exhaustive an understanding as is attainable of the human person to be educated.

The liberal arts, it is true, have been identified at different historical periods as galaxies of specific intellectual disciplines, and so they are. But in fidelity to the original inspiration of the Artes Liberales, each of these galaxies were derivative. They were, in a sense, relative and pragmatic and instrumental. They were judged, namely, to be arts befitting a free person. In short, the starting point to reconceive a meaningful liberal education should not be the islands and isthmuses of our intellectual disciplines, but an institutionally assumed assessment of the thrust and teleology of the free human person that is to be educated.

My judgment here is not simply the linguistic derivation of the term "liberal arts." This device merely reinforces the more fundamental judgment that a philosophy of education must depend upon and be conditioned by a philosophy of the human person. Yet in the broad range of colleges and universities in America, it is an understatement to say that clear and explicit philosophies of the human person have had little formative influence on efforts to conceive a viable liberal education. The absence has been, and until redressed will continue to be, crippling.

What arts, what activities, what forms of knowledge are befitting the free human person in today's American society? What activities performed will serve to fulfill and enrich the human person in today's American society? What ones, if omitted or unsuspected in their powers of satisfaction, will leave the human person empty, with potentiality stunted, with destiny unfulfilled? Certainly these are among the first questions colleges and universities genuinely interested in liberal education should be asking themselves, long before the questions of what fields enjoy favorable job markets, what major interest will have the greatest appeal for tomorrow's high school graduates. The fundamental task of the liberal arts college, therefore, is twofold: To assess for itself the meaning of human life--what leanings and latent stirrings of the human spirit are pointers to its fulfillment; and to create programs that will initiate and empower the burgeoning adult to follow these pointers.

To many, this task will seem an unreasonable burden. Yet however difficult or embarrassing, it is not unreasonable to ask a college to state its philosophy of liberal education. And without a philosophy of the human person, such a statement is an impossibility. What arts, what activities one judges befitting the free man or woman will depend upon what one conceives to be the free person's fulfillment.

It is obviously not possible to attempt to set out here a full blown philosophy of the human person. The task will appear simpler, however, and its inescapability more evident, from examples of two options that spontaneously arise in assessing the distinctiveness of the human person. Globally speaking, and in terms of overall priorities, rather than of detail, will the human person's fulfillment be realized in excellences of intellect or of freedom? In primordial thrust, is the human person a thinker or a doer? Or, indeed, is thinking a form of doing, of which there are other equally important types? Is the final measure of the fullness or emptiness of a human life to be found in what one has thought, or in what one has chosen to do?

Before the reader interjects that the dichotomy is too simplistic or allows his Christianity or his Americanism to speak for him, let us hear how Aristotle replied to the question over 2,000 years ago:

> To judge from the lives that men lead, most men and men of the most vulgar type, seem to identify good or happiness with pleasure...For there are, we may say, three prominent types of life: the life of pleasure; the active, political life of virtue; and thirdly, the contemplative life.

I cite Aristotle not only because of the clarity and precision with which he ultimately situated activities of speculative intelligence as human fulfillment, and therefore profoundly affected the intellectualist tradition of the Western world, but also because he posed for all succeeding culture the vexing problem of how highly to esteem the evident values embodied not in contemplation, but in the free pursuits of citizenship, the pursuits of justice and love, in choices inseparable from political and commercial and professional and personal careers.

In short, I personally believe that colleges and universities today, if they are to fulfill their obligation of providing an education befitting free persons, have to develop, as institutions, an institutional response to the great questions that have been crystallized in the classic discipline that we call ethics. Colleges and universities must pose, not merely to their students, but to themselves as institutions, the question that was framed by Aristotle, by Kant, and in our own day more recently by Albert Camus. For Aristotle, the question of ethics expressed itself as the search to discover wherein human happiness lies, in what types of activities, as I just mentioned, whether those of political life, of contemplative thought, or those attractive precisely because of their pleasure. For Kant, the question was expressed as the simple: What is worth doing? What ought a human person do? And for Camus, the question dramatically posed was that of suicide; whether or not life has meaning.

If colleges and universities, as institutions, would not merely create curricula in which individual philosophers could address these questions, but could once again, as institutions, express their judgment with regard to what does constitute human happiness (what sorts of appreciations, in what mixture of intellectual, aesthetic, affective, political, economic, religious activity, is the human person to find his or her good), I believe the colleges would not only be able to assist students more effectively to make choices, but they would find a nucleus of a response to two of the most urgent problems that are currently their own.

Kant framed the problems with which he dealt in three different questions: What can one know? What is worth doing? What can man reasonably hope for? If a college or university can institutionally measure how high the hopes of a human person can reach, can express its conception of human fulfillment, can determine what is worth a person's choosing, it will have a new principle of selectivity for what is worth knowing. As long as colleges continue to construct and reconstruct their liberal education programs exclusively out of the raw materials of ever-expanding disciplines, their principle of unity will continue to be increasingly vague.

I believe that if enabling persons for sound choices--economic, social, political, religious, ethical--is regarded not as an accident, but as the stated goal and final test of a liberal education, we would have a new and fruitful and ever-changing center around which to select what our several institutions believe is worth knowing out of the expanding universe of our disciplines. And we would have, indeed, what liberal education has most needed since Daniel Bell wrote twenty years ago: a new principle of unity to give sense and direction to its program.

TRANSMITTING THE WESTERN HERITAGE
THROUGH EDUCATION

by Russell Kirk

Let us not claim too much for formal education. In its original signification, the word "education" seems to have meant a kind of peripatetic and casual instruction, given to a child by a person assigned to lead that child outdoors for a walk; while a "pedagogue" appears to have been, in classical times, of a condition not much higher than that of a male nannie, fit for a little but imparting some rudiments of learning to the little boy who strolled beside him, hand in hand.

I commence my remarks in this disparaging fashion because nowadays many folk abase themselves before the image of Holy Educationism. We are informed by the cult's publicists that a barbarism worse than that of the old Mongols or Turks would descend upon America, should a teachers' strike be permitted to extend for more than a fortnight; we were warned by voices more doom-filled than Cassandra's that if the Reagan administration were to reduce even slightly federal expenditures upon loans for college students, posterity would curse us for having blasted forever the works of the imperial intellect. You may surmise that I detect charlatans in the numerous temples of Holy Educationism. Nay, I go so far as to declare that much of what we call Education, with a capital E, is no better than a racket and a boondoggle. In the course of thirty-five years, I have visited some five hundred college campuses. In my salad days, I assumed innocently that all these institutions were bent upon developing right reason and moral imagination. But of recent years my illative sense has informed me otherwise. Now I suspect that were I to put most college administrators and professors to the question, "For what purpose does your institution of higher learning exist?"; and were I able to extract from my victims perfectly candid responses--why, the general answer would be, "Our institutions exist to furnish employment for administrators and professors; all else is incidental."

So when we discuss the passing of a cultural heritage from generation to generation, ages to ages, we need to remind ourselves that the school--the higher or the lower school--is but one of the instruments employed in this complex task. Social custom looms larger than does formal schooling in the perpetuation of any culture--even so complex a culture as ours has become. The family, too, matters more than does the school in this labor: which is a reason why the thriving of family life ought to take precedence over expansion of the frontiers of the Educationist Empire, now aspiring to reign over countless day-care centers, it being impossible to lure more students to colleges. Much of a culture is transmitted by training, as distinguished from education--that is, by apprenticeship, internship, and learning-by-doing; formerly nearly all crafts were so acquired and passed on to the rising generation. If by "education" we imply the existence of regular teachers and schools, it is quite possible for a culture to dispense altogether with education--although not, perhaps, a high and complex culture.

So let us be modest in our claims for what education does. For all that, formal education remains in our civilization an important means to ensure that generation may link with generation. But what is this heritage that education ought to transmit?

I am supposed to be talking about a "Western" heritage, according to the title assigned to me; but I object to that title. This term "Western civilization" is a creation of the twentieth century, disseminated by such historians as Arnold Toynbee and by the dull authors of duller textbooks for hideous college survey-courses in the history of world civilizations. The term leads us to such absurdities as the theory that Western civilization exists in New Zealand, but Eastern civilization exists in Romania.

In reality, the civilization of which we in America are heirs is "Western" only in the sense that in part it arose slowly in western Europe--though in part only, and not in western Europe alone. You and I live in what Sir Osbert Sitwell called "this lying age." (He referred to daylight-saving time.) Were we candid, we would speak not of "Western civilization," but of Christian civilization.

I emphasize this point because it is necessary for us to know what sort of heritage education endeavors to transmit. The heritage of Saint Thomas More is not the heritage of Jeremy Bentham, even though both of those men spoke a form of the English language and lived in London.

This particular question arose in 1957, when I was participating in an international conference on North Atlantic community, held at Bruges. What joined together the states whose governments adhered to the North Atlantic Treaty Organization? Was there not some bond among them that was more than temporary military expedience? The Conference did examine seriously the foundations of a common civilization. But the members did not attempt to define precisely the common patrimony of Europe and America; there would have been too much squabbling at the outset, had such an attempt been made; it was assumed that some common heritage of moral principle, of culture, and of social institutions still subsists.

Prudently the Conference refrained from drawing up any such abstract document as the United Nations' Universal Declaration of Human Rights. This lack of precision, however, had the disadvantage of leaving unuttered the beliefs that had commanded the loyalty of most people on either side of the Atlantic.

In his closing address to the Conference, Paul-Henri Spaak, the Belgian politician, got briefly to the heart of the matter. (Spaak, you may recall, was the Social Democrat who succeeded in depriving Leopold III of the Belgian throne.) He declared that the unifying element in the North Atlantic community of nations was Christianity. But Spaak hastily qualified this doctrine by adding "as enriched by humanism and the French Revolution." Now humanism in one form--that of Erasmus and More--did enrich Christianity, although probably that was not the form of humanism which Spaak had in mind. But the French Revolution did nothing to Christianity except to kick it downstairs. This equivocation from a politician usually unequivocal was a concession to the rationalists and egalitarians present at the Conference, but it suggested an ambiguity which necessarily afflicts the search for common ground in the Age of Ideology.

To be honest, the culture to which we are heritors, and which we ought to endeavor to transmit to those who will succeed us here below, is what Chateaubriand called "the genius of Christianity." I do not employ the term "Judeo-Christian heritage": that is more equivocation. It is perfectly true that ancient Israel and Judah taught mankind much, and that by agency of Christian civilization, for the most part, the Hebraic perceptions were disseminated throughout the world. I have much emphasized this influence in my book *The Roots of American Order.* But it does not follow that Judaism and Christianity are one thing, or that we need to hyphenate the name for the civilization in which we have our being. If we were to hyphenate adequately, indeed, we would find ourselves referring to our Judeo-Hellenic-Roman-Muslim-Cartesian-Benthamite-Christian civilization: for there have occurred many grafts upon the trunk of Christian culture.

Our basic heritage, I am saying, is the patrimony of Christian culture. Culture is not the same thing as dogmata. It is not necessary to be a Christian communicant to share, and indeed to prosper, in Christian civilization. Those who dissent vigorously from the predominant culture nevertheless are born into that culture, enjoy certain of its benefits, and are powerfully influenced by it even when they denounce that culture most vehemently. If, with Voltaire, we deny that Christian culture exists--why, we do no more than engage in dialectic of the absurd. One thinks of an aside by James Thurber: "Had there been no Voltaire, it would not have been necessary to invent one."

The literature of Europe and America, the philosophies, the natural sciences, the laws, the arts, the mores--all are intimately bound up with the genius of Christianity. Hebraic, Hellenic, and Roman sources of thought and institution also are significant; yet they have survived chiefly as incorporated within a Christian civilization, and promulgated by Christian educational institutions--at least until recent decades. No living continuity of Hebraic or of classical culture survives to our time. The Jewish continuity was broken in the first century of the Christian era; the Roman continuity was broken in the sixth century, never to be restored. In the West, Christian civilization begins with Gregory I, at Rome; in the East, earlier, in the fourth century, with the successors of Constantine. When we speak of a "heritage," presumably we mean something that still lives and breathes and has its being: not of parchment merely. So we must perpetuate the heritage of Christian culture, or perpetuate no heritage at all. Even Marxism is a heresy from Christianity, retaining marks of its origin along with hideous disfigurements. It may be that, as some writers argue, we are entering upon a post-Christian era, in which there will rise up a culture and a civilization radically different from the civilization of the past fifteen centuries. But civilization as yet unnamed and indescribable (except in such dystopias as Huxley's *Brave New World*) does not yet provide us with a heritage. If we are concerned for the traditions of civility, the acquirements of science, the arts and the amenities, for wisdom and for virtue--why, it is the Christian heritage of culture which we must conserve and renew, whether or not we are ourselves Christians.

When I speak of the Christian heritage of culture, I do not mean "Christian values." In discussions about education nowadays, we may hear a great deal about "teaching values" in schools. This whole notion is a mistaken concept, although held usually by sincere people who mean well.

For what true education attempts to impart is meaning, not value. This sly employment of the word "value" as a substitute for such words as "norm," "standard," "principle," and "truth" is the deliberate work of the doctrinaire positivists, who deny that any moral significance of a transcendent or an enduring character exists. In America, the notion of educational "values" has been advanced by sociologists and educationists of the Instrumentalist school: it is intended as a substitute for the religious assumptions about human existence that formerly were taken for granted in schools. A "value," as educationists employ the word, is a personal preference, gratifying perhaps to the person who holds it, but of no binding moral effect upon others. "Other things being equal, pushpin is as good as poetry," in Bentham's famous phrase. Choose what values you will, or ignore them all: it's a matter of what gives you, the individual, the most pleasure and the least pain.

Etienne Gilson points out that positivists deliberately advance the concept of "values" because they deny that words, or the concepts which words represent, have real meaning. Thus the word "honor" may hold value for some, but may be repellent to other people: in the view of the positivist, the word "honor" is meaningless, for there is no honor, nor yet dishonor: all really is physical sensation, pleasure or pain. But if "honor" has an illusory value for you, employ it; if you dislike "honor," discard it.

I lack time here to develop this point. But perhaps I have said enough to suggest that the positivists' concept or word "values" distinctly is not part of that heritage of Christian culture which some of us are struggling to maintain and to advance. Every schoolchild used to be familiar with the catalogue of the seven cardinal virtues and the seven deadly sins. The positivists and a good many other folk today deny the existence of those seven deadly sins, or of any sin. As for the virtues--why, they would like to convert those into "value preferences," with no moral imperative to back them. But justice, fortitude, prudence, and temperance are not "values" merely; nor are faith, hope, and charity. It is not for the individual, bound up in self-conceit, to determine whether he prefers justice or injustice; it is not for him to decide whether prudence or imprudence suits him better. True, the individual may so decide and act, to others' harm or to his own harm. But it is the function of education to impart a moral heritage: to teach that the virtues and the vices are real, and that the individual is not free to toy with the sins as he chooses.

No, it has not been the purpose of genuine education of a Christian character to transmit "values". What true education transmits is a body of truth: that is, a pattern of meanings, perceived through certain disciplines of the intellect. Such education aspires to touch upon ultimate questions--from which the positivistic educationist flees. The sort of education which prevailed in Europe and America until fairly recently was an endeavor to instruct the rising generation in the nature of reality. It traced a pattern of order: order in the soul, order in the commonwealth. That old system of education began with information; it passed from information to knowledge; it moved from knowledge to wisdom. Its aim, I repeat, was not value, but truth.

This argument that the genuine education of Christian culture transmits meanings, rather than values, may surprise some persons who have been eager to restore a moral character to the curricula of schools. Those persons may be puzzled additionally by my refusal to identify values with virtues. What! Then has true education nothing to do with the formation of good character? Is education so concerned with meanings that it ignores morals?

Nay, not so. One approach to the meaning of human existence is the study of what Aristotle called "intellectual virtue." Moral virtue, the Greek philosophers came to recognize, was the product of habit, ordinarily acquired in family and community; but intellectual virtue--that is, conscious apprehension of good character by an intellectual process--might be developed and improved through systematic instruction. That is as true for us as it was for the Athenians.

We must not expect public schools, or any schools, to impart a high degree of moral virtue: that must be the effort of family, church, voluntary associations, even of the notorious "peer group." But we should call upon the schools to resume their old honorable task of acquainting young people with intellectual virtue--that is, the understanding of right conduct that may be derived from regular disciplines of the mind. A school cannot very well form good moral habits, having its pupils within walls only a limited number of hours in a week, and then under artificial restraints. Yet schools may do much to wake the moral imagination--which is another path to the apprehension of meaning.

But let it be understood that the imparting of intellectual virtue is a complex process; it is much more than a matter of uttering platitudes in classrooms. People who seek to restore the moral aspects of schooling frequently call for abrupt reform and speedy results. One well understands this demand; one sympathizes with the exasperation of many a parent on encountering the vulgarized positivism which has flowed out of teachers' colleges for more than half a century.

But the process of restoring meaning and moral purpose to formal education necessarily is a difficult one, requiring time. I do not mean that it is a hopeless task. What once has been may be again.

Over fifteen centuries, there was developed an educational pattern, altering with the passage of the years and yet retaining an essential character, that was meant to transmit Christian culture from generation to generation. This mode of education survived Renaissance and Reformation, and in some ways was invigorated by those movements; it persisted, little challenged, well into the nineteenth century; it was strong still, within my own time, at the older British universities. But today everywhere that venerable pattern of education is obscured, at best; often it is broken and derided. The French and the Italians have abandoned it, in effect, during very recent years. Public educational authorities in Britain have greatly injured the old educational pattern, deliberately, during the past quarter of a century. In America, the assault upon the old normative schooling became intense during the 1920s and 1930s, and by this time has triumphed almost everywhere. Quite as the Christian churches are in disarray and disrepute, so the aims and methods of imparting Christian culture are fallen upon evil days.

The Benthamite and Deweyite educational structure of our day, little concerned with meaning, aims confusedly at personal advancement, technical training, sociability, socialization, custodial functions, and certification--not to mention fun and games. The very possibility of ascertaining the meaning of anything is denied by many a department of philosophy. What does this twentieth-century educational system--if system it may be called--transmit to the rising generation? Chiefly certain technical and commercial skills, together with that training in the learned professions which is indispensable to our civilization. Modern schooling, at any level, offers very little toward the ordering of the soul and the ordering of the commonwealth. Yet neither the person nor the republic can long endure unharmed, if education continues to ignore reason, imagination, and conscience--or treats those three as objects of antiquarian interest merely.

Impediments at law in this land, together with the hostility or the indifference of a great many folk who style themselves intellectuals--the "Knowledge Class" described by Peter and Brigette Berger, to speak more accurately--make most difficult the restoration of an education that would seek truth rather than values. For that matter, many surviving church-related schools have succumbed to those intellectual fallacies of positivism and utilitarianism which are the enemies of Christian culture.

Yet if there is no education for meaning, life will become meaningless for many. If there is no education for virtue, many will become vicious. The American public begins to sense these unpleasant prospects: thus slowly opinion shifts toward such proposals as tuition tax-credits and voucher plans, which might make possible the survival or even the regeneration of a schooling founded upon Christian culture.

Indeed there remains a heritage worth transmitting--a patrimony indispensable, indeed, if our society is to be something more than a devil's sabbath of whirling machinery. Whether we Americans near the end of the twentieth century still retain sufficient intelligence and virtue to accomplish such a labor of restoration--why, that event is in the hand of God. That we talk, such as this one, of such possibilities, may hearten us somewhat. We Americans possess the riches and the power that could give us an American augustan age. Do we possess mind and heart requisite for an augustan era? It has been said that the Americans of our time know the price of everything and the value of nothing; it might better be said that they know the price of everything, the value of some things--and the meaning of next to nothing. We have not schooled ourselves, this past half-century and more, for augustan responsibilities; often, it has seemed, most American have forgotten that life has meanings beyond getting and spending.

So far as we remembered our heritage of culture at all, most of us Americans assumed that somehow it would endure automatically, unregarded and unrenewed--a form of perpetual motion. But that heritage has been fading among us for several decades. In educational fad and foible, in arid specialization, in mere processes of certification for potential employment, we have laid waste our inheritance of reason and imagination. At least some of us now know what devastation has been wreaked. There comes to mind a passage from Cicero's *De Re Publica:*

> Long before our time, the customs of our ancestors moulded admirable men, and in turn these eminent men upheld the ways and institutions of their forebears. Our age, however, inherited the Republic like some beautiful painting of bygone days, its colors already fading through great age; and not only has our time neglected to freshen the colors of the picture, but we have failed to preserve its form and outlines.

Have we now the sort of education that produced the Framers of 1787? Who so pretends? Do we school men and women in truth and virtue as did America's little country schools and simple colleges two centuries ago? The question is rhetorical merely. Yet unless one argues that the American people have decayed genetically, it remains possible for us to renew, through strenuous efforts, that sort of education for mind and heart--not precisely the same schooling in all details, of course, but nevertheless a schooling that would give precedence to vigor of understanding and to moral worth. But we cannot long delay this labor of radical conservation.

Little recognition of the cultural heritage that education transmits is to be encountered in A *Nation at Risk,* the report of the National Commission on Excellence in Education some years ago. What that influential report chiefly reproaches is intellectual sloth; it scarcely touches upon the fallacies that have enfeebled American schooling. For renewal of mind and conscience through education, we must pass beyond the recommendations of the National Commission, valuable although some of those recommendations are.

The sort of education that prevailed without much challenge until the nineteenth century sought an ethical end through an intellectual means. The generations of scholars who contributed to that pattern of education were well aware that a high culture is a product of art, not of nature; and that it must be nurtured, for the intellectual and moral qualities of humankind are menaced always by overweening will and appetite. The primary instrument of that pattern of education was great literature--taught as rhetoric, "the art of persuasion, beautiful and just"--and through other disciplines.

The scholars who formed that pattern of education knew, too, that what we call the present is merely a film upon the deep well of the past. The evanescent present vanishes as I speak; my words of a quarter of an hour ago have become part of the past; and the future is unknowable. It is from understanding of the past, chiefly, that meaning is derived and some measure of wisdom becomes attainable. Those men and women whose education almost excludes knowledge of the past are condemned to what T.S. Eliot called "the provincialism of time."

Lacking a good apprehension of the heritage of our civilization, we are forced back upon a rude pragmatism in private life and in public, a groping for "what works"--or seems to work. In private existence, such servility to the evanescent moment leads to the alienist's couch and the divorce court; in the affairs of nations, such naive improvisations (ignoring history) may end in ruinous blunders, not to be undone.

The education of yesteryear was founded upon certain postulates. One of these was that much truth is ascertainable; another, that religious truth is the source of all good; a third, that we may profit by the wisdom of our ancestors; a fourth, that the individual is foolish, but the species is wise; a fifth, that wisdom is sought for its own sake; a sixth, that true learning cannot be made easy; a seventh, that for the sake of the commonwealth, schooling should quicken the moral imagination.

Those postulates have not ceased to be true; it is only that they have been forgotten in our century's obsession with power and money, and our century's illusion that ideology is a ready and satisfactory substitute for thought. Some eyes have been opened to the mischief done by that obsession and that illusion. Here and there, some attempts at recovery of the true ends of education are being made.

I attest the rising generation. Educate yourselves, ladies and gentlemen, for self-education may suffice when formal schooling is sunk in decadence. Seek for meanings, ask yourselves ultimate questions. Then among you may spring up, in defiance of today's climate of opinion, those healthy modes of thought and imagination that were not born yesterday.

Turn conjurors, if you must, and raise up the spirits of the poets and the Schoolmen. You are the heritors of many centuries of thought and experience; if that inheritance has been denied to you in schools, still it may be gained privately. To exist without knowledge of the past is to dwell in a Flatland, lacking perspectives, without warmth, mystery, depth, memory, or justifiable hope. Many in America and throughout the world have been disinherited of their cultural patrimony. Yet they may win back that high inheritance, if they have fortitude and tenacity sufficient. "The dead alone give us energy," we are told by Gustave LeBon. In the long run, the man and the state that have rejected the legacy from many centuries will be found nerveless. And the man or woman who has sought out that legacy will be emboldened to defend the permanent things against Chaos and old Night.

LIBERAL EDUCATION, ORIGINALLY AND TODAY

by David Lowenthal

The idea of liberal education originated with Socrates, Plato and Aristotle as an intrinsic part of their moral and political philosophy. Ever since, it has retained--at least until recently--some recognizable features of its Socratic ancestry. Generally speaking, this meant some connection with what has long been referred to as "classical education," entailing the study not only of Greek and Latin but of the great works of literature, history, ethics and politics produced in these ancient tongues. In this tradition, classical education did not aim primarily at the education of philosophers but at the education of good men who were citizens or statesmen. Concentrating on human affairs, it always had a practical bent, and never lost sight of the fact that it anticipated, for those receiving it, an active rather than a contemplative life, a life combining political activity and leisurely pursuits. It aimed at affecting character, taste and intellect together, shaping the whole soul because the good life involved the whole soul.

The greatest sources of the idea of liberal education are Plato's *Republic* and Aristotle's *Politics,* and these works reveal important divisions and alternatives within that idea. The *Republic* introduces education as the means of making sure that the soldier-guardians of the city Socrates creates do their job well. For this purpose it is nothing but moral and political education, and to a large extent takes place at an early age. But the education of those who can go on to become the rulers--the philosopher kings and queens--of this society is primarily intellectual, and it alone is described, literally, as a *liberation* from servitude to the opinions of the city. Potential philosopher-rulers must be wrenched free and helped to seek the fulness of a truth that is trans-political and that at first has little bearing on the requirements of ruling. So attractive, in fact, is this search for universal truth that the philosophers must be *compelled* to return to their duties as rulers. Their wisdom--which is their primary title to rule--ends up being practical as well as theoretical. Their ties to the city, while temporarily suspended or forgotten, are once again resumed and, from that point onward, sustained. However reluctantly, they end up being as political as the soldier-guardians they command.

While the tradition of liberal education has sometimes leaned with Plato toward stressing theoretical wisdom, this has not been its usual course. The alternative view, stressing the life of the citizen and the gentlemanly use of leisure, has its roots in Aristotle's *Politics*, where the term "liberal education" first appears prominently. But the context in Aristotle is far from simple. The term occurs within his discussion of the best polity, just after his claim that such a polity must aim at the best life for human beings as such, allowing the good man and the good citizen to coincide. The best life, or the good life simply (he goes on to say), entails the superiority of peace to war, of leisure to business, and of the noble to the merely useful. Liberal education is the preparation of the citizens of the best polity for what most befits free men or gentlemen: the peaceful use of leisure in noble activity pursued for its own sake. Cultivating the love of the beautiful per se is an example of such education.

This view of liberal education contains, and masks, a deep ambiguity. By sharply distinguishing between business and leisure, while insisting on the superiority of leisure, it apparently separates liberal education from "business"--a term that includes not only one's own business but the business of the polity, and hence the entire realm of politics itself, in peace and war. Liberal education would have nothing to do with such matters-- with politics any more than with personal finance, for example. This has the general effect of consigning practical action as such to the sphere of "business," and along with it the moral virtues defined in terms of practical action, and best exhibited in it. It even overlooks Aristotle's earlier description (in the *Ethics*) of certain moral virtues as aiming at the noble for its own sake, and, by implication, degrades even these to the level of the instrumental--i.e., to being a part of business engaged in for the sake of leisure and the activities of leisure. Following this line of reasoning, liberal education, on the one hand, and moral or civic education, on the other, end up being sharply different things, with the latter inferior to the former. This does not mean the citizens in the best polity would fail to receive a moral and political education preparing them for the "business" that must in all cases precede and support "leisure." But it would simply that such an education could not be considered "liberal" or on a par with liberal education.

The *Politics* ends abruptly and incompletely, without failing in the upper levels of the education to which all citizens are to be exposed in the best polity. The upper levels will involve "music," a term that would be understood to include poetry. But what form will the poetry take, and will theoretical philosophy be included as well? Aristotle was intent, like Plato, on asserting the superiority of the very highest elements in us to those involved in our necessities, but there is little sign of any intention to educate a whole citizen body in theoretical philosophy. This means that the best polity cannot fully adopt what is best for man as such. In fact, Aristotle obviously seeks to restore a dignity and elevation to the realm of the practical that had been weakened, if not lost, in Plato, where it had been absorbed into the theoretical. After all, the *Ethics* and the *Politics*, taken as a single treatise, were meant to become the most significant part of the gentleman's moral and political education. Their almost exclusive concern is with the realm of practice--of business, action, peace and war. For practical reasons, this realm cannot be portrayed as simply subordinate to the higher ones of poetry and philosophy, even if its sole purpose was to supply the conditions that make them possible. Moreover, its disproportionately greater risks, rigors and opportunities may actually call forth higher human exertions than those involved not in philosophy or poetry per se but in the gentlemanly appreciation of them. In any case, for the sake of preserving the precedence of the practical life, Aristotle might have approved of the way John Milton defined education centuries later: "...I call, therefore, a complete and generous education, that which fits a man to perform justly, skillfully, and magnanimously, all the offices (duties), both private and public, of peace and war."

In nineteenth century England, liberal education had found a place between educating philosophers, aloof from political life, and directly preparing citizens or statemen for action in their own society. Using classical writings as its foundation, it had settled, more or less, on educating the good man--the man of moral and political virtue--in accord with Milton's definition. Such a man would be expected to participate in ruling, and to use his leisure for the study of human affairs, the appreciation of the arts, and, in lesser degree, philosophy or science proper. To this general training it would not be difficult to add whatever further training in the particulars of one's own society might be necessary for political action.

No one, of course, emphasized more than Aristotle the distinction between the good man and the good citizen, from which it followed that each political order was to educate not the good man generally but the good citizen of its own society. Aristotle also insisted that civic education inculcate virtues offsetting the destructive tendencies that each imperfect society typically called forth in its members. This principle had the effect of bringing the education of the good citizen closer to the education of the good man as such, despite the diversity of political orders. At any rate, the tradition of liberal education may be said to have concentrated on training the good man, and its various activities and studies were understood in this light. Literature, for example, had several uses simultaneously: to engender a love of the beautiful, to cultivate the moral virtues, and to convey a general instruction in human life necessary to wisdom. History, ethics and politics, undertaken as general studies, had similar purposes. And the same can be said for the activities out of the classroom or study that contributed in an important way to the nurture of human excellence.

Little remains of classical liberal education today. From the late eighteenth through the early twentieth centuries, the great educational debates took place around the inclusion within education of the new ideas of philosophy and science that began to dominate the intellectual world. Today the educational practices designed to produce both the good man and the good citizen are gone. The college curriculum now has a totally different orientation based on the academic disciplines. Liberal education is universally understood in terms of a general sampling of academic disciplines, combined with majoring in a particular discipline, on the one hand, and taking additional free electives, on the other. Such education is still proudly--too proudly--distinguished from practical, professional, occupational or technical education, but mainly by virtue of the broad sampling of disciplines it requires.

The disciplines are almost always thought to fall naturally into three discrete categories: the natural sciences, social sciences and humanities. But the basis for this tripartite division is rarely discussed. Its fundamental premise seems to be the distinction between sciences (meaning modern sciences) and non-sciences. By implication, the sciences are understood to be the exemplars of human knowledge--particularly the natural sciences, with the social sciences imitating them and seeking constantly to legitimize themselves as sciences. All disciplines that have no hope of becoming modern sciences are cast into the catch-all bin of the humanities: language and literature, the fine arts, history and philosophy. Occasionally religion itself is placed in this category, despite the obvious difficulty of calling something a "humanity" that claims to be not human in its derivation but divine--a "divinity."

In an age when science claims to be the model form of knowledge, all of the non-sciences can only make dubious claims to knowledge. This includes philosophy itself, formerly the queen of the sciences, but now relegated to a place indistinguishable from that of the arts, despite the different faculties of mind they involve. So, none of the humanities today can claim to speak with the voice of knowledge or the authority of truth, and hence give truthful guidance to human life. Nor do the institutions of higher education themselves stipulate the ends of life toward which the education they supply is intended to give guidance: on the contrary, they typically assume that, apart from becoming generally knowledgeable, the student must create or supply his own ends. Education thus understood has no direct connection with life: lacking in practical direction, it is both non-practical and impractical. Partly to fill the void of this aimlessness and serve as an anchor of sorts, majoring is introduced to occupy a substantial proportion of collegiate education. It requires the student, moved either by vocational expectation or personal bent, to choose one or possibly two subjects to major in. Thus, what is by the system's own definition of liberal education an anti-liberal (specialized) element is added to the liberal element of discipline-sampling and general knowledgeability.

It would not be too far from the truth today to say that the humanities are the last refuge of classical liberal education, battered and misshapen by the pounding blows of modern philosophy and science. Historicized, specialized, rejecting values for facts, imitating the precision of the sciences, even the humanities tend to lose their unique traditional capacities for education in human excellence. The resulting education, overall, is both intellectually narrow and excessively intellectual. At its center is one kind of knowledge--modern science--more or less dominating all the disciplines. At its periphery are the older and less precise but humanly more important "pretenders" (as we have come to think) to knowledge, and the appreciation of the elements of the soul, including virtue and beauty, that are not simply intellectual. This ultimate product of modern Enlightenment treats the student at best as a disembodied seeker of universal scientific knowledge, unrooted politically in any particular society. It would thus come as no surprise to find that the American college often renders its students less prepared to live responsibly as citizens, more susceptible to irrational ideologies appealing to idealism, morality and heroism, more inclined to succumb to forces outside themselves. The diverse parts of their soul have been attuned to no natural harmony, and they have been trained to be neither philosopher, citizen nor man.

The way out of this impasse has always been at hand. We must again begin to think of education as a practical art designed to produce a certain kind of human being, a certain set of human and political excellences, a certain way of life and action. Much of what is necessary to such an education we still have: the books, the natural inclinations and aspirations they appeal to, even some memory of the tradition of classical education lingering on in some faculty members and some written recollections. Above all, there is the sense these books immediately engender, by well-nigh universal consent, that they address the most important human questions, and in a way not only unmatched but unapproached by education today. Let those in every college who sense the necessity of such an education be gathered together and asked to form a program that can at least be offered students as an alternative to the present curriculum. With the help of such a lifeline we should be able slowly to pull ourselves ashore.

LIBERAL EDUCATION AND EDUCATION FOR CITIZENSHIP

by Christopher Bruell*

The title of my paper, whether by design or accident, poses a question, a problem: liberal education and education for citizenship--are they the same or not, and if not, what is their relation? Let's call liberal education education simply or strictly speaking, or its highest form, such education as aims at the formation of the best possible human being, or at guiding those capable of it to the discovery of the truth, of those truths most important to human beings as such. What is the relation of education so understood to education for citizenship? The reason why they are not simply the same education is clear. As Aristotle tells us, what a good human being is is the same everywhere, at every time so to speak. This is also what the Bible tells us: "He hath shewed thee, O man, what is good; and what doth the Lord require of thee, but to do justly, and to love mercy, and to walk humbly with thy God?" (Micah 6:8) The admonition of Micah is addressed to man as such; it is intended to have universal validity. But what it means to be a citizen--what rights and duties citizenship entails, what purposes the loyalty of citizens serves--all of this varies from country to country insofar as the forms and purposes of government vary. And therefore, as we also learn from Aristotle, what it means to be a good citizen varies from place to place--so much so, that in some situations, all too familiar in this century, it is impossible to be both a good citizen and a good human being at the same

---

* The author dedicates this essay to Allan Bloom, for his unrivaled contributions to higher education in America.

time. In those situations, education for citizenship is deeply at odds with the requirements of education strictly speaking, as is shown most strikingly by the prominence of pseudo-scientific doctrines of various kinds in the education schemes of certain countries. We recognize this state of affairs when we use the term "indoctrination" and distinguish what it designates from true education.

But nothing, that is, no pressing necessity, forces us to dwell on the relation of liberal education to education for citizenship in those extreme cases. We live under a good and decent form of government. What is the relation of liberal education and citizen education in the case where citizenship itself is something decent and admirable? By thus narrowing our question, we free it from most, but not all, of its difficulties. Before taking up thematically some of the positive contributions which, in this case, each sort of education has to offer the other, it might be worthwhile to cast a glance at the difficulty which remains. Its character is indicated by the contrast between two stories in the *Memorabilia* or "Recollections" of Xenophon. These "Recollections" are in fact recollections of Socrates, the citizen-philosopher and educator par excellence, Xenophon's own teacher and friend. I'll tell first the story which involves Socrates and Glaucon, who is familiar to us as Plato's brother and as a leading figure in Plato's *Republic.* When Glaucon was not yet twenty years old, he thought it was time to take the crucial step on the road to fulfilling his ambition to become leader of Athens: namely, to begin to speak out in the Athenian assembly. None of his friends or relatives could stop him from the attempt, which could result in nothing other than his being dragged from the speaker's platform, an object of ridicule. But Socrates brought him to his senses by means of a conversation which went roughly as follows:

> After securing the youth's attention by praising his ambition in extravagant terms, Socrates said, Isn't it clear, Glaucon, that since you wish to be honored, you must benefit the city?
>
> Certainly.
>
> By the gods, don't hold back but tell us where your good work in the city's behalf will begin!
>
> At this, Glaucon was silent. He had, obviously, up to that moment, never given any thought to where he would begin.
>
> Socrates had to help him out: Well, just as in the case of a friend's estate--if you wished to enlarge it you would try to make it richer--so in the case of the city, will you try to make it richer?
>
> Certainly.

76

Wouldn't it be richer if its revenues were to increase?

Probably.

Tell us then how many sources of revenue the city has now and what they are. Clearly you have looked into this, so that if some of them are not providing what they ought, you can remedy their deficiencies and if more sources are needed you can provide them.

But, by Zeus, these at any rate are things I have not looked into!

Well, if you have neglected these things, tell us at least what the expenditures of the city are: clearly you intend to cut the unnecessary ones.

But, by Zeus, I haven't yet had the leisure to look into those either.

Well, shall we put off making the city richer then? For how can anyone ignorant of its expenditures and revenues supervise these things?

But, Socrates, it is possible to enrich the city at the expense of its enemies [in other words, through war].

Socrates replied that this is indeed possible, providing that the city is *stronger* than its enemies. If it is weaker, on the other hand, it stands to lose rather than gain from war.

Glaucon conceded this.

Tell us first then about the city's power on land and sea and then about the power of its enemies.

But, by Zeus, I wouldn't be able to state it for you just like that, from memory!

Well, if you have it written down, produce it; I would be extremely pleased to hear about this subject.

But, by Zeus, I haven't yet written it down either.

Then war too we will hold off giving our advice about at first. For perhaps, because of the magnitude of these matters, you have not yet examined them at this the outset of your leadership. But surely you have already concerned yourself with the safeguarding of the countryside, and you know which of the guardposts are critical and which not and how many guards are sufficient. And you will advise us to

77

enlarge the critical posts and to cut the superfluous ones.

Glaucon's response appeared to be somewhat rash. Socrates asked him therefore whether his view was based upon an inspection on the spot.

It is an estimate, rather.

Well, here too, shall we give our advice only when we possess knowledge, not merely estimates?

Perhaps that would be better.

When it came to light that Glaucon had not gone to inspect the silver mines, either, an important source of state revenue, Socrates suggested that he might be intending to offer the excuse that the place was said to have an oppressive climate. Regarding the food supply, however--that is, the relation between Athens' annual production and its annual requirements--there could clearly be no excuse for failing to acquire the necessary knowledge.

But Glaucon protested: you are talking of an immense task, Socrates, if it will be necessary to supervise even things like this.

Socrates was now ready to bring the conversation to its conclusion: One can't be a fine manager even of one's own estate unless one both *knows* what it needs--everything that it needs--and takes care to supply all those things; and the city consists of more than ten thousand estates; since it is a difficult thing to supervise all of these at once, why don't you first attempt to enlarge one estate--namely, your uncle's, which needs it--and if you can do *this* , *then* try to supervise more? If you can't benefit one, how would you be able to benefit many?

But I *would* benefit my uncle's estate, if he would listen to me.

So, you are unable to persuade your uncle, but you think you will be able to make all the Athenians, your uncle included, listen to you? Watch out, Glaucon, lest desirous as you are of fame, you meet with the opposite. Haven't you observed how dangerous it is for one who lacks knowledge to speak or act...If you wish to be famous and admired in the city, try to acquire knowledge regarding those things you wish to do. (III, 6)

Thus Socrates reminded Glaucon of the range and magnitude of the responsibilities of a public leader and led him to see what sort of knowledge is needed to carry out those responsibilities in a competent manner. In doing this, Socrates fulfilled his own responsibilities as a citizen and a friend--though it is perhaps also fair to note that he did not offer to supply Glaucon with the necessary knowledge; it is even possible that he did not possess it in every case.

The other story concerns a conversation of a quite different tenor. It too involved a youth "not yet twenty" years old, one named Alcibiades. The conversation took place, at Alcibiades' initiative, with his guardian, who happened to be the renowned Pericles, the great leader of the Athenian democracy, then at the peak of his fame and power. It thus did not directly involve Socrates, but Xenophon includes it in his "Recollections" because, at the time it took place, Alcibiades was still a close companion of Socrates; in fact, the conversation revolved around the sort of questions Socrates himself was always asking. In other words, the Socratic influence--in however distorted a form--is unmistakably present in it.

> Tell me, Pericles, would you be able to teach me what law is?
>
> By all means.
>
> By the gods, teach it then. For when I hear people being praised as law-abiding men, I think that anyone ignorant of what law is wouldn't deserve this praise.
>
> In wanting to know what law is, Alcibiades, you don't desire anything difficult: whatever the assembled multitude approves [remember here that Pericles is the leader of a democracy] and puts in writing--declaring what must and must not be done-- all these are laws.
>
> Does the multitude believe that the good things or the bad must be done?
>
> The good by Zeus, boy, and the bad must not be done.
>
> And if it is not the multitude but, for example, where the government is oligarchic the assembled few put in writing what is to be done--what are these things?
>
> To which Pericles replied: All that the dominant part of the city, upon deliberation, puts in writing regarding what must be done, all that is called law.
>
> Even if it is a tyrant who is dominant in the city and who puts in writing for the citizens what must be

79

done--are these things law?

Even what a ruling tyrant puts in writing, even those things are called law.

To which Alcibiades responded: But force and lawlessness--what are they, Pericles? Aren't they found whenever the stronger compels the weaker--not persuading him but through use of force--to do whatever the stronger decides?

That's my opinion at least, Pericles said.

Then, whatever a tyrant compels the citizens to do, not persuading them, and puts in writing--is this lawlessness [rather than law]?

In my opinion it is, Pericles replied, for I retract my former answer to the extent that it held that what a tyrant puts in writing, without using persuasion, is law.

And what the few put in writing, not persuading the many but exercising dominion over them--shall we or shall we not say that these things are force [rather than law]?

In my opinion, Pericles said, everything that one compels another to do without persuading him, whether he puts it in writing or not, is force rather than law.

Then whatever the whole multitude puts in writing, not persuading the rich but exercising dominion over them--would these things be force rather than law?

At this point, Pericles ceased to answer Alcibiades but said to him instead: You know, Alcibiades, we too, at your age, were very sharp in discussions of this sort; we practised them and played the sophist as you now appear to me to practise them.

To which Alcibiades replied: O that I had known you when you were at your sharpest, Pericles. (I 2.40-46)

Now, to bring our two stories together: nothing further, at least nothing bad, was heard of Glaucon. Socrates had apparently restored him permanently to the path of responsibility and good citizenship. But Alcibiades--an equally close, in fact a closer companion of Socrates than Glaucon was--became the most notorious traitor of his age, doing irreparable harm to Athens in the process; even prior to his treasonous activity, he was conspicuous for the lawlessness of his private behavior.

Now it would be foolish and unfair to blame Socrates for all of this; but it is, also, difficult to be certain that his undoubted influence on Alcibiades was entirely harmless. I draw the following simple, but perhaps far-reaching, conclusion from the stories: while liberal education has an important contribution to make to education for decent citizenship, and while, as we will see, the converse is also true, liberal education should not be thought to be identical with education for citizenship even in the best case of citizenship in a decent community. Even here, at a certain point the paths of the two sorts of education diverge, for the one culminates in the raising of questions which, for the most part, it is not necessary to raise for the purposes served by the other. It would probably be a disservice to both sorts of education to fail to respect their distinctness, just as it would be to fail to recognize their indissoluble connection.

Let's turn then to that connection--more precisely to some aspects of the contribution which liberal education can make to education for citizenship in our country, taking liberal education now to mean the education which is or ought to be available in our colleges and universities. The citizens who can be expected to come in contact with this education will be especially leaders or rather potential leaders of their communities. What attributes would qualify them to exercise such leadership? Turning to Aristotle's *Politics* (v. 9) for an answer, we find that he mentions these: friendship toward the established form of government; capacity for the great tasks of office; and virtue, including the sort of justice upheld by that particular form of government. That liberal education as we are familiar with it has some contribution to make to the development of such qualities is clear, I think; that there are certain limits to its contribution is perhaps also clear. For example, the role of church and family and of education at the primary and secondary levels in the development of moral virtue and of loyalty toward American democracy is clearer than the role of liberal education here, and almost surely more important. No amount of so-called higher education is likely to be able to make up for what is lacking at earlier stages; rather the usefulness of the higher education may well presuppose the effectiveness of what has come before. To mention just one point, there is an emotional bond to our country and what it stands for that must, in most cases at least, precede and accompany further education in its political principles if that education is to have its greatest impact. With regard to capacity for great tasks, to take another example, liberal education can point out, as Socrates did to Glaucon, the various sorts of knowledge necessary for the accomplishment of those tasks; given the current constitution of our universities, it can even supply much or all of that knowledge; but it is more difficult to say how, and even whether, it can contribute to the development of prudence--the judgment which enables one to *use properly* the otherwise merely technical knowledge. The difficulty here is due partly to the fact, which Aristotle points out, that the development of prudence presupposes the presence of moral virtue--to take just a small but not insignificant example, the courage to look harsh facts in the face without blinking or turning aside. We could make liberal education our sole reliance for the development of prudence, then, only if we could make it our sole reliance for the development of moral virtue. Here again its utility depends to some extent on what has gone before, as well as on the presence of a suitable nature.

Nevertheless, the utility of liberal education--both in the development of prudence in those who have the capacity for it and in the development of an educated devotion to American democracy--is far from negligible. To turn first to prudence or judgment, this cannot be *taught*, strictly speaking, not only for the reason already given but also because it does not consist solely in having, and holding on to, the right opinions. There are no infallible rules that can simply be memorized or mastered and then applied--rules, for example, that would let us determine when it is or is not proper to take an action involving risk to life. Nor are there rules to guide the gathering and absorption of the myriad bits and pieces of information necessary to informed decisions--still less rules to insure the correct assessment of the information available so as to yield accurate estimates of an opposing leader's character, for example, or his influence. But liberal education can help by fostering the habits of observation and reflection which are integral elements of prudence or judgment. The unsurpassable model in this regard is Thucydides' history of the twenty-seven year war between Athens and Sparta, a work which is designed to make of its reader almost a participant in the great political events narrated in it. As a quasi-participant, the reader is all but compelled to make judgments and decisions as the actual participants did: Should the Athenians make an alliance with the Corcyraeans as the speech of the latter in the Athenians assembly urges; or should they refrain from doing so as the answering speech of the Corinthians insists? What information is relevant to the decision, and what is available; what considerations of right or interest should guide it? Thucydides confronts his readers with such questions in scores of concrete situations, giving them as much but generally no more information than the actual participants possessed at the time the choices had to be made, the actions taken or abstained from. And he rarely obtrudes his own judgment to relieve the reader from the task of thinking for himself and thus developing the habits of observation and reflection referred to. But the education which Thucydides' history and similar works provide in this way may make a still more significant contribution to the development of prudence. If prudence does not consist solely in the possession of the right opinions, it can be impeded by false opinions which pose obstacles to its development even where the other requisites are present and which thus distort the capacity for judgment of good and bad men alike. To clarify this notion of *obstacles* to prudence, it will help to give a few concrete examples. The first is from Thucydides--a passage toward the end of his account of the Sicilian expedition, the unsuccessful Athenian attempt to conquer Sicily and thus begin to expand their empire to dimensions later achieved by Rome. With their cause in Sicily clearly lost, the Athenian generals made a much-delayed decision to withdraw their army and navy from the island and thus prevent defeat in Sicily from becoming defeat in the larger war with Sparta: for it was difficult to see how Athens could hold out in that war if she should be deprived of the forces then in Sicily, the cream of her military strength on both land and sea. The generals' decision came at the last possible moment for the Athenians to get away; the enemy forces on the spot were gaining strength daily and were eager to inflict a crushing defeat on the Athenian force before it could escape. When preparations for the departure were complete, and the Athenians were on the point of leaving, there was an eclipse of the moon. (Thucydides remarks that the moon was full; he seems to have made a point of noting when such things occur.) At this Nicias, the general with the greatest authority, declared that he would not even consider departing before waiting "thrice nine" days, as the diviners were advising (and the bulk of the soldiers--but not the other generals--was urging). Thucydides is sufficiently moved by this decision, which sealed the Athenians' fate, to permit himself a rare comment: "Nicias was somewhat too inclined toward divination and such things." A more recent example comes from Churchill's reflection (in *The Gathering Storm*) on what might have led the responsible ministers to the grave error of judgment constituted by the Munich agreement with Hitler. As Churchill emphasizes in the narrative leading up to the reflection, Chamberlain did not believe that the peace purchased at such a price would last even three months:

> It may be well here to set down some principles of morals and action which may be a guide in the future. No case of this kind can be judged apart from its circumstances. The facts may be unknown at the time, and estimates of them must be largely guesswork, coloured by the general feelings and aims of whoever is trying to pronounce. Those who are prone by temperament and character to seek sharp and clearcut solutions of difficult and obscure problems, who are ready to fight whenever some challenge comes from a foreign Power, have not always been right. On the other hand, those whose inclination is to bow their heads, to seek patiently and faithfully for peaceful compromise, are not always wrong. On the contrary, in the majority of instances they may be right, not only morally but from a practical standpoint. How many wars have been averted by patience and persisting good will! Religion and virtue alike lend their sanctions to meekness and humility, not only between men but between nations. How many wars have been precipitated by firebrands! How many misunderstandings which led to wars could have been removed by temporising! How often have countries fought cruel wars and then after a few years of peace found themselves not only friends but allies!
>
> The Sermon on the Mount is the last word in Christian ethics. Everyone respects the quakers.

> Still, it is not on these terms that Ministers assume their responsibilities of guiding states. Their duty is first so to deal with other nations as to avoid strife and war and to eschew aggression in all its forms, whether for nationalistic or ideological objects. But the safety of the State, the lives and freedom of their own fellow countrymen, to whom they owe their position, make it right and imperative in the last resort, or when a final and definite conviction has been reached, that the use of force should not be excluded. If the circumstances are such as to warrant it, force may be used. And if this be so, it should be used under the conditions which are most favourable. There is no merit in putting off a war for a year if, when it comes, it is a far worse war or one much harder to win. These are the tormenting dilemmas upon which mankind has throughout its history been so frequently impaled. Final judgment upon them can only be recorded by history in relation to the facts of the case as known to the parties at the time, and also as subsequently proved. (Churchill, *The Gathering Storm*. Boston: Houghton Mifflin, 1948, pp. 285-286.)

The choice of these two examples may have left a misleading impression. It goes without saying that neither the sole nor, in our time at least, the gravest obstacles to prudence have their source in an insufficiently educated piety. That source is much more likely to be the one indicated in the final example, taken from some reminiscences of Trotsky regarding Lenin. (*On Lenin: Notes Towards a Biography*) The remarks in question concern some theses written by Lenin in January of 1918, where he seems to regard the success of socialism in Russia as requiring only a few months. Trotsky wonders whether Lenin could have meant seriously these and other similar, apparently unrealistic statements: *"He believed in what he was saying.* [This is emphasized in Trotsky's text.] And so the fantastic date for socialism--six months hence--testified also to the same Leninist spirit which showed itself in his realistic approach to every immediate task. The deep and unyielding conviction that there were tremendous possibilities of human development for which one could, one should pay the price of suffering and sacrifice, was always the hall-mark of Leninism." It would be difficult to put the matter in a nutshell better than Trotsky does--one might only wish to add that the sacrifices Lenin referred to were, of course, to be made by others.

If certain false opinions, for example the opinion that there are possibilities of future human development so tremendous as to justify the inflicting of unspeakable suffering on the present generation in order to bring them about--if false opinions of this sort are obstacles to the development of a humane and truly prudent judgment, then liberal education can make a contribution to the development of such prudence by combating them, by showing us how the world is, the world God gave us and must expect us to act in, by calling our attention to the permanent features of the world we know. This is what' Thucydides does. He is sometimes compared in this respect to Machiavelli, who regarded his superiority to ancient political philosophy as consisting in his greater realism. But Thucydides shows us the way the world is not, as Machiavelli does, to shock and ultimately overcome our attachment to justice but rather to educate and refine it. To this end, his severe but beautiful prose first calls forth that attachment and nourishes it: he continually invites us to judge the participants in the history and their actions, both nations and individuals, in moral terms. But he insists in return that we familiarize ourselves with all of the relevant features of the situation in which the actions we judge must be taken, all of the features which moral judgment must take into account if it is to be truly moral. To recall an example mentioned earlier, would the Athenians be in violation, as the Corinthians claim, of an already existing treaty if they make an alliance with the Corcyraeans? And if this is the case, are the defense requirements imposed by an impending and all but unavoidable war sufficient to excuse such a breach of their word? Or, to take another example, is a small nation to be condemned for taking Athens' side in her wars of expansion and thus helping to enslave her neighbors? What were the concrete choices available to that nation at the time? Does a truly moral course of action require that one possess the strength to be independent? What, in turn, are the foundations of such strength? Properly used, Thucydides' work provides an education in the unchangeable necessities that limit all possibilities of human development but also, for that very reason, provide the arena within which truly moral action and judgment is possible and needed. And the works of Aristotle, among others, do the same. When we turn for example from the end of his *Ethics* to its sequel the *Politics*, we are likely to do so with the expectation and hope that we are about to learn how to increase vastly the amount of virtue in the world through the use of appropriate legislation. Read from this perspective, the *Politics* comes to sight as the gentle but thorough and relentless account of the difficulties preventing the fulfillment of that expectation; it is the required political education of the moral man. It is intended, like Thucydides' book, to foster a manly acceptance of what cannot be changed, while at the same time--and only in this way-- encouraging the calm but determined effort to do that which can be done.

To turn just briefly now to the place of liberal education in the development of an educated devotion to American democracy, I think it is clear that at each stage of learning, the pre-existing bond of attachment to country must be deepened by the learning appropriate to that stage. At the college level, this would include the assiduous study of the fundamental documents of American democracy as well as the writings of those who have reflected most adequately on our politics and way of life. The Declaration of Independence, The Constitution, the Federalist papers, and writings of Washington, Jefferson, Lincoln and deTocqueville would be included on any such list. This study would be significantly assisted by attention to some of the great philosophic teachers of modern republicanism, Locke and Montesquieu especially. One additional point needs to be mentioned. In the same chapter of the *Politics* in which he puts "friendship toward the established form of government" first among the attributes desirable in a leader, Aristotle also says that education in the spirit of the regime is the greatest of the means of preserving a particular regime (or form of government). Then, however, he adds remarks to the effect that the intention of such education should be to foster a moderate or sober, rather than an extreme attachment to the spirit or principles of the government. The reason, which he develops at length elsewhere in the *Politics*, is that the principles of any actual government can never be free from flaws. The unbending application and extension of them, while gratifying to extreme partisans, is likely to undermine, in the long run, the very survival of that form of government by making the government worse. An educated attachment to American democracy must include, then, awareness of its blemishes and flaws--not those which are held to consist in the insufficiently rigorous application of its principles; rather it is the principles themselves which have to be looked at in this light. And for this purpose, the use of the writings of the non-democratic thinkers (I don't say anti-democratic, but non-democratic) of our past, of the philosophic tradition, is probably indispensable.

In conclusion, I want to mention just one contribution which the concern with education for citizenship can make to liberal education--but an essential contribution, at least in my view. When we turn to the generally old and difficult books which must constitute the core of a true liberal education, we are confronted too often with the situation that guides to help us uncover their riches are lacking. For whatever reasons--some are not too hard to seek: it is much easier to specify the training of a competent physicist than that of a competent interpreter of Shakespeare--this is often our situation. And that means that we have no other guidance than what is supplied by our own seriousness. That is, it must be the seriousness of our purpose in seeking out these books which grants us some access to their contents. And it is dfficult to think of a more serious purpose than the desire to develop in oneself or another the capacity for a sort of high citizenship. It is when we turn to the old books with our political and moral concerns foremost in mind--to learn more about justice and war, about the strengths and weaknesses of various forms of government, about the temptations and dangers of tyranny--it is when we do this that these texts cease to speak to us in an alien, if charming, idiom and begin to speak instead in plain terms of matters which touch our lives and concern our role as citizens and our place in the world.

LIBERAL EDUCATION AND THE PUBLIC MAN

by William M. Bulger

In any response to the request that I would speak about my own personal education in the liberal arts as being valuable in my political life, it seems to me that it is only right to say at once that I consider myself to have been fortunate. Having grown up in South Boston, I had the opportunity to attend Boston College High School, Boston College, and Boston College Law School, and I was especially fortunate to do so at a time before the Jesuits had abandoned their famous code of liberal education known as the *Ratio Studiorum*. This was an orderly plan of studies in the liberal arts of grammar, logic, and rhetoric, having, as its distinctive viewpoint and method of approach, the use of pagan classical authors, not precisely for their own intrinsic interest as writers of poetry, oratory, and history, but for their aptness to serve as models for pupils to emulate in their own similar compositions. I was thus introduced early to a tradition of studies in the liberal arts, in accord with a special philosophy of education, and for this I am, and must ever remain, grateful. It was, in fact, even more, for it was an introduction to a humane culture of the distinctively human faculties, founded on a unified, twofold base, both of the ancient pagan classics and of Christian philosophy and theology, and it had the specific aim of developing the natural human talents of the pupils and of inculcating in them virtuous habits of life, thought, and action.

I say, then, that I was fortunate. Yes, for it could all have been different--in fact, less satisfactory. I might never have been exposed to the influence of the great minds of classical antiquity. After all, there are millions of Americans who have not had that good fortune--millions who have no intimate familiarity with the achievements, for both good and evil, of past ages and civilizations--millions who are, in fact, intellectually rootless. I was fortunate in this, that, by no special merit of mine, I was enabled to enter into that great literary and historical tradition, and, at least in some degree, to capture its essence and strive to make it my own personal possession, operative in my life, my legal career, and my public service in both legislative chambers of the Commonwealth of Massachusetts.

Having learned the ancient Greek language at Boston College High School and having studied the Greek text of the *Anabasis* and the *Iliad*, I entered Boston College well equipped to pursue advanced studies in Greek literature. There, first and foremost, I encountered Demosthenes, whose power I have not forgotten and cannot forget. At once I recognized his power of thought, and I felt his power of expression, for he had a mastery of argument and of emotion that I was happy to emulate. There was a man who gave of himself unsparingly to the common good of his country. There was a man who adhered to principle and who relied on common sense in his statesmanship. There was a man who meant what he said and said what he meant. Yes, and there was a man who, when fortune was unkind, knew that he had done his best, and had done it unselfishly. My admiration of Demosthenes was unbounded.

Now you understand that I was only eighteen when I met this great man. But what a stirring meeting it was! What a splendid example for a young man in America who already had at least some vague political ideals and interests! The impact on me was incalculable. How fortunate I was to be thus led into the very historical studies that had formed his statesmanship and devotion to his country, into the study of rhetorical art and persuasion that had made him his country's greatest orator, and later into the study of the ethical and political treatises of Aristotle, "the master of them that know."

Indeed, I would be inclined to say that the close and concentrated study of Demosthenes gave me an insight into, and a realization of, power in political life. Demosthenes, you see, was well aware of the autocratic power of Philip of Macedon. That was despotic power, tyrannical power, irresponsible power--in fact, totalitarian power, as we would probably call it today. To such power Demosthenes had no claim, no access; actually, it was repellent to him. His was only the power of persuasion, his the power of personal integrity.

It seems to me that the whole long history of mankind, at least insofar as I know it, witnesses, broadly speaking, to these two kinds, or manifestations, of power: that in which there is, and that in which there is not, respect for the dignity of the individual human person. Despotic control in civilizations of great masses of men has always been the preferred method for the use of power. Only in exceptional situations has the common man been considered worthy of controlling his own destiny. I could perhaps say that the stark contrast between the views of Thomas Jefferson and of Alexander Hamilton parallels that intellectual abyss between Demosthenes and King Philip. In his *History* Herodotus makes exceptionally clear the contrast between the huge oriental monarchies, where all are slaves except the Great King, and the tiny city-states of Greece, where there is, at least in theory, equality of man and citizen before the law.

It is, to be sure, easily seen that the early American colonists held views that crystalized in the Declaration of Independence. Jefferson never claimed originality for the content of that document, and he was too modest to claim what was rightly his, the masterly style of expression in which he clothed that content. These are, of course, ultimately Greek views on the dignity of man, and, while they have had a long life, that life has been limited to severely restricted areas of the world. Even in America today there are, I fear, clear signs that large numbers of people among us no longer hold them in full vigor, but would gladly bargain them in exchange for some form of economic security--which is, of course, ultimately delusive. There is no sound reason to imagine that "mass man" in modern America would be likely to be better off than "mass man" in ancient Assyria or Persia.

So I am led, in a sort of roundabout way, from my retrospection on the literary aspect of my education to a few thoughts on its second major component, the Christian view of the human person and his innate dignity. This is the study of human nature, first, in an abstract way by the light of natural reason, and, second, by the aid of supernatural revelation. It is a study of that composite species of being known as man, together with its natural consequences and requirements in the moral order, the social sphere, and the political community. This abstract philosophical study is complemented by consideration of what divine revelation tells us of the fall of man by original sin and of his restoration to friendship with God the Creator by Christ the Redeemer.

From these studies in philosophy and theology the Greek view of the intrinsic dignity of the human person is seen to be solidly based. Recall Hamlet's paean of praise:

> *What a piece of work is a man, how noble in reason,*
> *how infinite in faculties, in form and moving how*
> *express and admirable, in action how like an angel, in*
> *apprehension how like a god: the beauty of the*
> *world, the paragon of animals...*
>
> (II.2.312ff.)

One can only marvel at the perspicuity of the lonely, unaided ancient Greeks. They could so easily have been overwhelmed by oriental darkness, by the savage barbarity of their neighbors on every side. They could have been crushed by the unlovely, totalitarian views that had come down to them from earlier and more powerful civilizations. But they struck out for themselves. They thought their own thoughts and came to their own conclusions. To their utmost power they squared their views with reality. Then, to top it all, not only did they bring to birth outstanding works of art and literature, but also they bequeathed to us a political culture which is still fruitful centuries later and in an opposite hemisphere.

Thus in my education the pagan liberal arts of grammar, logic, and rhetoric had their counterpart and complement in the rational sciences of philosophy and theology. The truths attained in these studies were the solid substructure of my study of Anglo-American law. I do not, because I cannot, accept the view that force, or coercion, is the basis of law. In my view, if law is not founded on justice, on the right relation of persons and things, it has no ultimate binding power, Although it may be imposed for a longer or shorter while, enlightened human nature cries out against it, condemns it, and rebels against it. I have, therefore, accepted the traditional view of jurisprudence, and it has sustained my grasp of the principles of right on which alone legislation can be firmly based. These principles have informed my research into all the myriad questions and proposals that have arisen in my more than twenty-five years of public service in our legislative chambers.

I am not, indeed, the first to pay tribute to Demosthenes and other noble Greeks who are an honor to our common human nature, and I hope I shall not be the last. I know that Jefferson acknowledged his debt to them, and I know that Dr. Samuel Johnson believed that every one should get as much Greek as possible. Although I am well aware that few of my contemporary Americans share my views, I shall continue to hold them until I see overwhelming evidence against them. As I said at the beginning of this essay, I consider that I was indeed fortunate in the liberal education I experienced, and I wish very sincerely that others may be, in their turn, equally, or even more, fortunate.

In conclusion, I think I may be allowed to say that, even had I gained nothing else from my education in the liberal arts, I have firmly embraced the principle enunciated in chaste elegiac verse by Solon, the great Athenian legislator: γηράσκω δ᾽ αἰεὶ πολλὰ διδασκόμενος --which is: *"I grow old ever learning a lot."*

THE EDUCATIONAL THOUGHT OF THE
FOUNDING FATHERS

by Ralph Lerner

Can one speak of the educational thought of the Founding Fathers? Those who proposed this topic to me assumed the answer to be yes. In accepting that assignment I apparently did not think otherwise, but further reflection on the matter now suggests some doubts. I am led to wonder whether the level of abstraction necessary to meld disparate thoughts and thinkers may not make that exercise less helpful and revealing than one might wish.

If we look back to the Founding Fathers of this country and try to sketch their understanding of education, we are apt to be struck less by their unity than by the diversity of their thoughts and proposals. This should not be surprising. Only a small proportion of those whom we call Founding Fathers left evidence of their thoughts on education, but that small number were among the more forceful, articulate, and purposeful of their group. Knowing their own minds and not having to grope for words to express their thoughts, those Founders tended to speak in ways that distinguished them from one another. It is, accordingly, easier to detect a variety of voices than a single call.

Nor is this the only obstacle to speaking globally and with confidence about the educational thought of the Founding Fathers. How large a net do we want to cast when we use that term? Obviously it would include Benjamin Rush, a signer of the Declaration of Independence and a founder of Dickinson College. Even more obviously it would include Thomas Jefferson, author of the Declaration of Independence and father of the University of Virginia. Ought it to embrace as well Jefferson's teacher, James Maury, who thought and wrote with considerable care about the kind of education proper for the young Virginians in his charge? Could it leave out that tireless proponent of a national government and a national language, Noah Webster? There is no need for me to list other names, equally or even more eligible for inclusion, in order to confirm the obvious. Those who might plausibly be connected with the founding of this country and who addressed their thoughts to the education of its youth had in view a broad array of moral, religious, and political expectations. That diversity is reflected both in their ends and in their choice of means.

None of this is to deny that almost everyone who had call to reflect on education in America took for granted that the special conditions of American life precluded a mindless aping of English models. With the advent of openly-proclaimed republicanism and political independence, the distinctiveness of American needs became even more evident--and urgent. So it was that devising an education that befit a new and rising people became a matter of conscious concern for a number of the Founders. The expression of that concern could take many shapes: a Benjamin Rush seeking to promote Christianity with a view to its strengthening republicanism; a Benjamin Franklin constructing an artful story of his life after which others might model their own coolly rational conduct; a James Madison attempting to induce the reluctant Virginia House of Delegates to enact Jefferson's Bill for the More General Diffusion of Knowledge; a George Washington seeking to foster a national university, which might overcome parochial passions by nourishing enlarged views and continental loyalties.

Given this rich diversity of means and ends, it might be more helpful to eschew the encyclopedic mode of treating this subject, where one can say only a little about a lot, in favor of a closer and keener look at a particular Founder. In choosing a restless ex-schoolmaster of Worcester, Massachusetts, as my point of focus, I do not mean to suggest that John Adams was a *typical* Founder--for there was no such animal--nor that his thoughts on education exhibit especial coherence and profundity. They do, however, show the intense interpenetration of moral, religious, and political concerns to which I have already referred. In this respect the opinions and actions of John Adams provide as good an entry into the educational thought of the Founding Fathers as we are likely to find.

No one would be surprised to learn that education (or, more generally, knowledge), is intimately connected with liberty in the mind of John Adams. This is, indeed, a persistent theme in his public and private writings, a leitmotif running from his earliest newspaper contributions through his Inaugural Address a third of a century later, and beyond. That theme might be restated plainly enough: there is no such thing as a passive citizenry. To the extent that a people view "the public administration of government" as a distant spectacle and not as a matter of intimate concern and consequence, they stand in jeopardy of being both demeaned and oppressed. "Let us not be bubbled then out of our reverence and obedience to Government, on one hand; nor out of our right to think and act *for ourselves*, in our own departments, on the other." But for Adams, exercising that right is not something that comes naturally; it presupposes a public that has been rendered qualified for its tasks. "It becomes necessary to every subject then, to be in some degree a *statesman*: and to examine and judge for himself of the tendency of political *principles* and *measures*."[1]

Knowledge is power: so the modern philosophers have taught. So, too, may the monopolization and manipulation of knowledge be power. In that respect we might do well to think of knowledge as a neutral force having the potentiality for liberating a people--or enslaving them. At any rate, it was clear to Adams that the failure of many generations to see through the fraud and violence of "the princes and nobles of the earth" and to shake loose of their oppression was owing in large measure to the people's ignorance. Deprived of the means by which they might come to have "knowledge of their rights and wrongs," the common people were for too long beset by a double battery of tyrannical rule. Ordinances that held them in "a state of total ignorance of every thing divine and human," and opinions that reduced "their minds to a state of sordid ignorance and staring timidity": these, Adams asserted, were the malicious consequences of the feudal and the canon laws.[2] In becoming aware of that fact, the people would be taking the first step toward their own liberation.

These simple truths were hardly mysteries to those whom John Adams looked back to as founding fathers. That "sensible people, I mean the *Puritans*," saw clear through the fantastical constructs that had been used to justify the doctrines of passive obedience and nonresistance. "They knew that government was a plain, simple, intelligible thing founded in nature and reason and quite comprehensible by common sense."[3] Their understanding and experience convinced them that only "knowledge diffused generally thro' the whole body of the people" could forfend the resurrection of those old tyrannies. Accordingly, they used "every measure, and [took] every precaution in their power, to propagate and perpetuate knowledge." They committed themselves and their posterity to supporting a system of education extending from college to the smallest village grammar school. "So that the education of all ranks of people was made the care and expence of the public in a manner, that I believe has been unknown to any other people ancient or modern."[4]

It would be a blunder to dismiss Adams's praise of Puritan principle and practice as self-congratulatory filiopietism. If anything, it would be truer to say that in his eyes it was this aspect of Puritan principle and practice that in fact justified his admiring those imperfect mortals. The deeper truth was that the people's rights and liberties could no long be preserved if that people were basically ignorant, self-absorbed, and corrupt. Adams took as a premise the proposition that education had something positive to contribute toward making and keeping a people fit to be their own best governors. With that in view, his draft of a constitution for Massachusetts proclaims it "the duty of legislators and magistrates, in all future periods of this commonwealth, to cherish the interests of literature and the sciences, and all seminaries of them...to encourage private societies and public institutions" for these and related purposes. All this is to the end that the people of Massachusetts may not only deal sociably with one another (no small achievement in its own right), but even grow capable of entertaining "generous sentiments."[5]

Nor was there any doubt in Adams's mind that "cherish" meant "pay for." Perhaps this can best be viewed as a matter of self-respect. Brave talk about the people's being the origin of all political authority would mean little if their exercise of their constitutive power were pitiable or contemptible. "The whole people must take upon themselves the education of the whole people, and must be willing to bear the expenses of it." At least as important as the fact that there be a school was that it be seen as a *public* charge. Thereby, Adams thought, the whole people would gain respect in their own eyes; they would "be taught to reverence themselves, instead of adoring their servants, their generals, admirals, bishops, and statesmen."[6] No more authentic display of popular "power and majesty" could be imagined than the continued existence of a free republican government. For that happy effect, President Adams thought, would bear powerful witness to its root cause--a people fit for self-governance. Here, at last, was a genuine object of national pride.[7]

A corollary of all this is that poverty would be no bar to "the liberal education of youth." Just as the founding fathers of Massachusetts had required that every town of defined size support a full-time schoolmaster, so too would Adams treat "the preservation of the means of knowledge, among the lowest ranks" as a public utility. Indeed, he did not hesitate to assert that the rich in particular had a special interest in the education of the poor, and "that to a humane and generous mind, no expence for this purpose would be thought extravagant."[8]

Despite this emphatic talk of public support for schools, Adams hardly limited his educational field of vision to those conventional means of instruction. Education would proceed on a broader front than the classroom and lecture hall. I would even go so far as to say that for John Adams (as for Thomas Jefferson), the greater part of a people's education would come not from school but from their active participation in their own governance. By this I mean more than that the people might learn from their mistakes, or that experience might perhaps make them wiser if sadder. Of all this, John

Adams says little. Rather, he stresses how a properly founded constitutional system "introduces knowledge among the People, and inspires them with a conscious dignity, becoming Freemen." He envisions a setting in which the usually divisive strivings of individual emulation and ambition might provoke more civil behavior.[9]

None of this bespeaks faith in some magical transformation of individuals or of the people as a whole. Rather, the thought and expectation refer to the enlarged opportunities ordinary and not so ordinary folk would have under republican institutions. The comparative advantage of New England--so obvious to Adams at the Second Continental Congress--turned in no small measure on its system of local government. He was quick to note how that system, "empowering Towns to assemble, choose officers, make Laws, mend roads, and twenty other Things, gives every Man an opportunity of shewing and improving that Education which he received at College or at school, and makes Knowledge and Dexterity at public Business common."[10] In short, political participation in and of itself contributes to an education. The great value of a popularly elected assembly is not only that it "gives free access to the whole nation" and gives voice to all its wants and wishes. Beyond that, it "affords opportunities of exertion to genius, though in obscurity, and gives full scope to all the faculties of man; it opens a passage for every speculation to the legislature, to administration, and to the public; it gives a universal energy to the human character, in every part of the state, such as never can be obtained in a monarchy."[11] Where James Madison held the protection of diverse human faculties to be the first object of government, John Adams held the enlargement and enlivening of those faculties to be the great object of republican education broadly conceived.

This sense of grander objectives, of goods that extend beyond political independence--indeed, beyond politics--is displayed nowhere more clearly than in the correspondence between anxious parents. Abigail Adams, left alone on the farm to provide for their children's education, was all too aware of her own inadequacies relative to her expectations. The lesson she drew was also clear: from now on, the education of American daughters could no more be neglected than the education of American sons. "If we mean to have Heroes, Statesmen and Philosophers, we should have learned women."[12] John could only agree; and when he, in turn, was left alone to provide for their sons' education Holland, he showed that he too had no little plans. He complained of his trouble in trying to find suitable schools for young Charles and John Quincy. "I should not wish to have Children, educated in the common Schools in this Country, where a littleness of Soul is notorious...There is besides a general Littleness arising from the incessant Contemplation of Stivers and Doits, which pervades the whole People." It was not that Adams held frugality or industry in contempt. He well understood how necessary close attention to expenditures might be in order to maintain one's independence. But the preoccupations of merchants and traders, and the rules by which they governed their behavior, were objects "that I hope none of my Children will ever aim at."[13]

More fitting for the younger Adamses would be those very subjects in which John Adams dared not now indulge. His rambles among the beauties and refinements of Paris and Versailles brought these thoughts vividly to his mind. "The Science of Government it is my Duty to study, more than all other Sciences: the Art of Legislation and Administration and Negotiation, ought to take Place, indeed to exclude in a manner all other Arts.--I must study Politicks and War that my sons may have liberty to study Mathematicks and Philosophy. My sons ought to study Mathematicks and Philosophy, Geography, natural History, Naval Architecture, navigation, Commerce and Agriculture, in order to give their Children a right to study Painting, Poetry, Musick, Architecture, Statuary, Tapestry and Porcelaine."[14] Once again, John Adams showed that the establishment of good government, however much the focus of his thoughts and energies, was but the means to a larger and more richly human life.

Notwithstanding the nobility and beauty of this vision, John Adams never let it distract him for long from an immediate concern with governance. His reasons are plain enough to see. Almost everything that might enlarge the soul and lend dignity to man still presupposed a political order; for without some auxiliary system of holding human prejudices, appetites, and passions in check, neither reason nor conscience could prevail. Left to fend for themselves, the most eligible plans for improvement and reformation would be hectored to death by the envious and ambitious. Adams believed that for all the good education might do, it still could not suffice against that brute fact, "the great and important melancholy Truth...that all Men would be Tyrants if they could."[15] Indeed, far from being sufficient to contain political dangers, education might make matters worse. In a defectively organized government--defective because too simple or "unballanced"--the "Influence of general Science" would be especially baneful. By raising the level of competence without correspondingly raising the level of character, education would be multiplying the "number of able and ambitious Men, who would only understand the better, how to worry one another with greater Art and dexterity." Nor would the heightened conscientiousness of religious men in such a flawed political setting ease the pain; their earnestness might only intensify their singlemindedness.[16]

As a result, Adams was impelled to return to his point of departure. By all means promote knowledge and benevolence as much as possible; but by no means count on "seeing them sufficiently general for the security of society." From first to last, he was intent on "seeking institutions which may supply in some degree the defect." To the extent that "knowledge, virtue, and benevolence" increased through education, mankind would be confirmed in belief in the good sense of the republicanism of John Adams. They, like him, would hold to "the opinion of the necessity of preserving and strengthening the dikes against the ocean, its tides and storms." Even a revolutionary people, hot for liberty, needed to be redoubled in their resolve to adhere to "the true principles." That necessary task would proceed by spreading "light" wherever possible and, "at least in the greatest number," by enlisting "prejudice, passion, and private interest...on the side of truth." Here, Adams thought, was a continuing field for the education and the educational efforts of the few and the many.[17] Perhaps this comes close enough to expressing the educational thought of the Founding Fathers: no one's needs could be ignored, no one's contributions could be spared.

The relevance of the Founders' thought to educating the man and the citizen in America today is neither obvious nor clear. They were, let us never forget, reared under a system of government they overthrew or radically revised. Those qualities of mind and pen for which we may admire them most also owed much to modes of thinking and interacting that the Founders' political success has rendered less likely or even unsuitable. Whether their political foresight also took in those kinds of changes, changes that would call for another kind of compensatory education, I cannot say.

More obvious to us and more fit for emulation by us is their keen awareness of the relation between political independence and general education, between the moral tastes (what we today might call the attitudes) of a population and their capacity to be and remain their own masters. Exhortation, indoctrination, and civic rituals might all make some contributions toward creating a public of fellow citizens, but for none of the Founders did those devices hold talismanic powers. At bottom, sound prejudices could support sound reasons, but prejudice and passion were no substitutes for reason. Accordingly, just as self-governance posed the greatest challenge to humankind, so would its success stand as the greatest compliment to the species. It is just shy of astonishing to reflect that those unsentimental Founders, intent on taking men as they are, nonetheless thought they had cause for hope. Their reasons for thinking so are still worth pondering.

Their grounds for hope had little or nothing to do with their adherence to a general philosophy of optimism, or with a belief in a benign human nature, or with a doctrinal assumption that Americans were somehow exempt from the historic failings of their forebears. These thumbnail characterizations of the men of '76 and '87, once beloved by textbook writers and their student readers, have little basis in reality--at least as far a the leading Founders are concerned. Nor was hope for their revolutionary project limited to the Jeffersonians among them, as distinguished from sour Federalists caught in their own net of paranoia and ideology. This is another tribute to the ingenuity of latter-day scholarship, but it too misses what the Founders themselves recognized as their common ground.

They agreed that Americans were no better than other human beings and yet had better opportunities than others had even imagined. Those singular

97

circumstances consisted as much in what was missing from America--what did not require overcoming--as in the positive qualities of men, land, and institutions. Together, they formed an unprecedented opportunity to show what might be possible for nonangelic men without benefit of special revelation. It was not a case of making a whole new beginning, going back as it were to the First Pair. Yet there was a possibility of making a new order of the ages and of doing so in a way that might serve as a model for those less fortunately situated and as an inspiration for those others to do better for themselves.

The education of the Americans was thus both a conservative task and a revolutionary challenge. By better preparing the people at large for their principal business--self-governance--, American education would at one and the same time be securing domestic tranquility and demonstrating that the cause of liberty was a practical ideal. In this respect the Founding Fathers were themselves teachers. By showing how considerations of self-interest might be joined to a philanthropic impulse, they hoped to teach their successors a useful lesson. The career of the American people need suffer from neither mean-spirited calculation nor grandiose futility. Learning how to avoid both of those extremes in the conduct of their domestic and foreign affairs would be a necessary lesson for each generation to master for itself.

NOTES

1. "U" to the Boston Gazette, no. 6, 29 Aug. 1763, in Taylor, Robert J., et al., eds., *Papers of John Adams* (Cambridge, Mass.: Harvard University Press, 1977), 1:80-81. (Hereinafter this edition is cited as "*Papers*.")

2. "A Dissertation on the Canon and the Feudal Law," no. 1, 12 Aug. 1765, *Papers*, 1:111-13.

3. *Ibid*, 1:114; "A Dissertation on the Canon and the Feudal Law," no. 2, 19 Aug. 1765, *ibid*, 1:117.

4. "A Dissertation on the Canon and the Feudal Law," no. 3, 30 Sept. 1765, *ibid.*, 1:118, 120.

5. The Constitution of Massachuesetts, 1780, chap. V, sect. II, in Adams, Charles Francis, ed., *The Works of John Adams* (Boston: Little, Brown and Company, 1850-56), 4:259. (Hereinafter this edition is cited as "*Works*.")

6. John Adams to John Jebb, 10 Sept. 1785, *Works*, 9: 540.

7. Inaugural Address, 4 Mar. 1797, *Works*, 9: 107-8.

8. "A Dissertation on the Canon and the Feudal Law," no. 3, *Papers*, 1:120-21; "Thoughts on Government," Apr. 1776, *ibid.*, 4:91.

9. "Thoughts on Government," *ibid.*, 4: 92.

10. John Adams to Abigail Adams, 29 Oct. 1775, in Butterfield,L.H., *et al* ., eds., *The Book of Abigail and John: Selected Letters of the Adams Family, 1762-1784* (Cambridge, Mass.: Harvard University Press, 1975), 112.

11. Preface to *Defence of the Constitutions of Government of the United States of America*, 1787, in *Works*, 4: 288-89.

12. Abigail Adams to John Adams, 14 Aug. 1776, *Book of Abigail and John*, 153.

13. John Adams to Abigail Adams, 18 Dec. 1780, *ibid.*, 282.

14. John Adams to Abigail Adams, post 12 May 1780, *ibid.*, 260. In fact, only in the fourth generation would there be a Henry Adams.

15. "U," nos. 6-7, *Papers*, 1: 79, 82.

16. John Adams to Benjamin Rush, 19 June 1789, in Biddle, Alexander, ed., *Old Family Letters*, Series A (Philadelphia: J.B. Lippincott, 1892), 39-40.

17. John Adams to Samuel Adams, 18 Oct. 1790, *Works*, 6:414-18.

EDUCATING THE MAN AND THE CITIZEN IN HIGHER EDUCATION

by Peter V. Sampo

The distinction between the man and the citizen is Aristotle's. In the Politics he states that the good man is not necessarily the good citizen; for if a man is a good citizen in a bad regime, he cannot avoid doing evil, detracting, thereby, from his humanity. It is only in a good regime that a good citizen is a good man.

How do we educate the man? How do we introduce the man to his humanity? By introducing him to Western culture. And by introducing him to Western culture we introduce him to America. In educating man and citizen, we have to look back to the founding acts, the founding of the West and the founding of America. It is in these acts that the substance of our tradition was generated.

Western tradition is a result of a certain kind of revelation, that found in the Old and New Testaments; a certain kind of reason, Greek philosophy; and a certain kind of symbolic imagination, found in Western literature, exemplified by Dante. In all three of these ways of expressing reality, emphasis is placed on the symbolic character of immanent reality. The immanent reveals the transcendent and one can approach the transcendent only through the immanent, no matter how tempting it is to try to somehow leap over the immanent and approach the transcendent directly. The transcendent is revealed in the immanent in the Old Testament through the paradigmatic history of Israel and in the New Testament by the Incarnation itself and by the resulting sacramental vision. It is in this understanding of the transcendent character of immanent reality that culture is generated. The work of culture is not simply "basket weaving", the problem raised by John Courtney Murray, i.e., passing time until things are consummated but it is the difficult though subtle work of Incarnating the transcendent in the immanent. It is difficult because the sacramental vision is a tenuous one, easily lost and it is a subtle one, easily slipping from the Baroque to the Rococo. The threat posed to this symbolic imagination is that of the gnostic religion, whether it be the ancient gnosis that Hans Jonas speaks of or that of modern gnosis so well described by Eric Voegelin. If ancient gnosis would have won out in its competition with Christianity there would have been no Western culture, only a desert. We can say this because wherever modern gnosis has prevailed, for example in Marxist countries, either there has been a cultural desert or what little culture has existed has been a remnant of pre-Marxist culture.

The task of educating the man in this tradition is quite difficult since to bring to the attention of the students the substance contained in the founding of the West runs against several intellectual currents. One current is the tendency to accept the Enlightenment view of history. Voltaire, who challenged Bossuet's updating of Augustine's view of history, saw Western history as the progress of the human spirit through extinction (the Middle Ages), renaissance (the period of Henry II) and his day of growing enlightenment. Similarly, Turgot saw history as the progress of the human spirit moving through the famous three stages of religious, metaphysical, and scientific, later developed in more detail by Auguste Comte. Any one of these views which are current coin of the intellectual realm serve to cut us off from the past. This severing of the person from his past results in not knowing who we are and what we are to defend and, indeed, not caring. Of what relevance is Plato to men who have come of age in the scientific tradition? But I daresay that if one has not read and taken Plato to heart, all the cries for justice in the world will bring about nothing but tyranny. If one has not read and taken Augustine to heart, then all the cries of peace will but lead to more enormous wars, as they did in the 1930's. Who today reads Plato and Augustine? To oversimplify Plato, one would say that justice is the result of everyone in the City minding one's own business. It is the business of the wise to rule so that the proper political end of the City may be brought about. None but the wise are permitted to rule, certainly not the soldiers, and certainly not the technocrats. Soldiers and technocrats, and, one might say, bringing Plato up to date, bishops do not know this maxim and scuffle for the right to rule and if successful pervert the purpose of the city properly understood. For Augustine, peace is the tranquility of order. Order is a result of justice. To believe that peace is possible in our time of ferociously unjust ideologies is to suffer the delusions that went into the Kellogg-Briand pact of 1928 that purported to abolish war. As one wag put it, thank goodness for the Kellogg-Briand pact or we would have had war in 1939. Taking Augustine to heart is needed to counter the trend of political romanticism in America about the nature of the world. But who reads Augustine? Not many college students and probably not many seminarians.

The second obstacle that hinders bringing to the attention of students the founding act of the West is the understanding that one can do without the symbolic imagination, a product of both the scientific revolution and the Enlightenment. Somehow, because science does not tend to understand itself as "looking through a glass darkly" but as directly seeing reality, all human endeavors which acknowledge the symbolic character of their work are not scientific and, therefore, are not worthwhile. This has resulted in attempts to make these endeavors worthwhile by making them scientific, for example, to make political science like mathematics or to count as philosophy only that which is "empirically" verifiable. Although it is to be acknowledged that these trends have lost their elan, the debris of this view is still with us in popular mentality and, above all, in education. The myth of the useful has just about gained the whole field of battle in higher education. Our curricula have turned into preparing young men and women for careers; that is, to make them useful for some commercial or industrial firm. This mentality at the least insults the businessman. A businessman leads a highly symbolic life. What businessman has not said, "The trouble with you idealists is that you have never had to struggle to meet a payroll!" What is contained in this sentence is an understanding of the heroic quality of leading the life of a businessman in a competitive and risk-taking society. It is this symbolic life of heroic adventure that produces wealth in America. It sounds strange to say but, nevertheless, it is true that from the symbolic emanates the useful. Without Shakespeare not many and not very good boots are manufactured. Formed by Christianity and Greek philosophy, it was the symbolic imagination of the West that founded science and technology. It is not science that founded and formed the West; it is a relative latecomer to the Western scene.

Where does America come in? America is a child of Western history. It is not a break with the West but a special development of the Western tradition. It is a product of the rediscovery of the Western political tradition in the wake of the break up of the universalism of Christendom, the illumination of the significance of the person by Christianity and the need for the adequate representation of the person, and the development of the rational science of politics as applied to political institutions as a remedy for the *amor sui* that threatened political existence in the seventeenth and eighteenth centuries.

America is a good result of the meeting of the challenge posed to political life by the chaos following the draining of the Christian substance of the Middle Ages brought about by the Reformation, the religious wars, and the growth of nationalism. Prior to these developments, the *homonoia* of the West was provided by Christianity and its universality represented by Pope and Holy Roman Emperor (a universalism that did not include the Eastern empire, the Far East, or even Scandinavia). With the breakup of this universalism, and with the growth of *amor sui*, the question became what can the nation-state provide in the way of spiritual substance for the heart and mind? More than one Western thinker attempted to substitute an artificial theology, a civil theology, for the real thing. One thinks of Hobbes and Rousseau. Later, there was Comte with his religion of humanity. In the field of action, there was Robespierre's cult of the supreme being. The approach of Rousseau and Robespierre was to see political activity as the way for man to lose his selfishness and as a way to a spiritual regeneration of man, thereby expecting far too much of political activity. There was the approach of Hobbes who saw that *amor sui* not only broke up the old order but provided the motive for a new order. Since man is monstrous, only a monstrosity in the form of a Leviathan can keep order. Hobbes expected too little of politics. Man is not able to achieve moral virtue in the Leviathan, only peace and order.

It will be remembered that Auguste Comte, in order to provide his future society with a basis for order, wished to instill in man the virtue of *amor altri*, i.e., altruism instead of *amor sui*, *amor dei*, according to Comte, having long ago disappeared as a basis for order. We must say that Comte was quite perceptive in recognizing that *amor dei* had disappeared as a source for order and that *amor sui* could not provide the order. He was less perceptive in his remedy, expecting that man would replace his other loves with altruism. After all, he should have recognized that Robespierre's attempt was in essence his own attempt.

It was Madison who solved the problem. As Madison tells us in Federalist paper #10, one should not attempt to abolish factions by abolishing liberty, for "liberty...is essential to political life...". To abolish liberty, then, would be an abolition of the political. What does he mean by the "political"? In paper #51 he tells us: "In the extended republic of the United States, and among the great variety of interests, parties, and sects which it embraces, a coalition of a majority of the whole society could seldom take place on any other principles than those of justice and the general good..." The properly political, for Madison, is that process by which the coalescence for justice and the common good takes place. And man has to be free to participate in that process--the very same freedom that permits factions. We can understand this if we hearken back to Aristotle. In the *Politics*, Aristotle states that the aspect of man that makes him properly political, unlike the social insects, is speech, which, Aristotle says, "sets forth the just and the unjust and the expedient and inexpedient." By permitting liberty, Madison permits factions but they pay a price. If they wish to move legislation, they have to speak about the justness of their cause if they are to gain a majority. In the extended republic since there are many factions, factions cannot simply act, they have to speak. They have to convince enough people to form a majority but a majority could seldom take place on any other principle than those of justice and the general good. This is to say two things: multiplicity of interests militates against forming an oppressive majority and that within the body of American people there is sufficient virtue for there to be a dispassionate recognition of justice and the common good. There is within the American people a sense that tells them what is just and unjust, what is common good and what is special interest. Where does that come from? While the institutions of representation, extended republic, and federalism may be institutional means of curing the mischiefs of factions, nevertheless if the sense of what is just and unjust is not present within the people there can be no cure for the mischiefs of factions and America will collapse into anarchy and tyranny as did the ancient republics. In separation of powers the *amor sui* supplies the defect of better motives in so far as the office is tied up with the person whose self-love will guard the privileges and powers of the office. But the argument for the beneficience of representation in an extended republic is that the representatives will be a "chosen body of citizens whose wisdom may best discern the true interest of their country and whose patriotism and love of justice will be least likely to sacrifice it to temporary or partial considerations." (#10) Whence this virtue?

Certainly the very institutions of politics, according to Madison, tend to lead men to virtue. Given fragmented governmental power, moderate legislation will result with the effect that it will tend to find a large basis of assent. It will be the moderate men who will come to power in this arrangement.

The two questions that a political theorist asks about a political society are: What is the relationship between the man and his society, that is, what attaches the man to the society? And what is the civilizational content of the society? What kind of activity predominates in the society? What Madison had in mind for the civilizational activity of America, what actually came to pass, is commerce. Madison had in mind a commercial republic in which not only is property widely held by the citizens but different types and amounts of property are widely held. This system has several advantages. One, there is no great division between the rich and the poor. Two, the wide variety of property serves to fragment interests into many factions. Three, free institutions nourish a certain kind of spirit. It is this latter that deserves some attention. In answer to the question of what will restrain the House of Representatives from making legal discrimination in favor of themselves, he answers, "the genius of the whole system; the nature of just and constitutional laws; and, above all the vigilant and manly spirit which actuates the people of America--a spirit which nourishes freedom, and in return is nourished by it." (Federalist #57) Free institutions go a long way to form the virtuous citizen. These institutions not only serve the purpose of encouraging the multiplicity of factions, which helps prevent an oppressive majority faction from forming, but they have the much more political aspect of nourishing political virtue, particularly vigilance and manliness. One may even say that American political and economic institutions by their very structure help form the participant in the virtue of prudence. It has often been pointed out that one of the key differences between the American and French revolutions was the fact of the experience

105

of the American leaders in political life and the inexperience of the French leaders. This lack of practical wisdom on the part of the French revolutionaries was disastrous and led to unrealizable political expectations. Regardless of what Barry Goldwater said, moderation in the pursuit of justice *is* a virtue. Our political and economic institutions go a long way to inculcate political prudence in our citizens.

Where is our leadership supposed to come from, according to our Founders? They are to come from the natural aristocracy, the existence of which both Madison and Jefferson are in agreement. Jefferson wrote to John Adams (October 28, 1813): "For I agree with you that there is a natural aristocracy among men. The grounds of this are virtue and talents." It is this diversity of talents whose purpose it is for the government to protect, according to Madison: "The diversity in the faculties of men, from which the rights of property originate, is not less an insuperable obstacle to a uniformity of interest. The protection of these faculties is the first object of government." (Federalist #55)

What kind of a formal education is suitable for a natural aristocracy in America? The same kind of education that is suitable for the free men of America. And what education is that? The traditional education of the West, is the answer, the one that has served the West so well and the one that formed our Founders, i.e., a liberal education. This is the proper education for both man and citizen. Although this liberal body of knowledge has been accumulated, renewed and defined over the years and is the particular heritage of universities, students do not receive this heritage automatically or accidentally. A deliberate effort must be made to convey the benefits of the tradition to its students. And it must be made in a renewed fashion if the current assault on liberal education is to be thwarted. Liberal education like civility is always endangered, above all in this present time. We educators must not lose the battle by default. The liberal arts tradition must be renewed. The formalism of the past, the emphasis on system at the expense of the love and excitement of learning should not be retained in renewed liberal arts education. Real renewal can only occur when liberal education is taken in its fullness.

Liberal arts tradition says that there is some knowledge that is too important to be known for any other reason than its importance for our own being. It is a kind of knowing that celebrates what is discovered and known. It is the kind of knowledge that enables the classroom to be a center of celebration and drama and the center around which the rest of academic activity revolves.

Liberal arts assumes a certain view of time. It rests upon a consciousness of a distinction between profane and sacred time. Profane time is the consciousness of the day-to-day necessary activity that has to do with a succession of moments. It is the view that there is a functional part of life that must be gotten through, that there are obstacles to be overcome, and one must set aside time and set one's mind to overcoming them. Liberal tradition rests in the consciousness that there is such a reality as sacred time, which is not day-to-day time, but a time made distinct from profane time. When we act in such a way or think in such a way that natural delight results, then that acting or thinking is rooted in the very nature of our being; and we have taken that moment out of profane time and made it sacred. When we transcend profane time, we are at leisure--leisure understood as that activity rooted in sacred time, as an activity of celebration not as an amusement or an ennui or time off. Indeed, the best example of leisure activity is activity at celebration, the activity of effortless effort that produces delight in the soul. The classroom in the liberal arts tradition is to be understood in a similar sense.* For an academic community classroom activity holds similar importance as the Mass does for a monastic community. It is in the liberal arts classroom where the celebration of knowing, the celebration of the significant, and the raising-up of sacred time reaches its completion. In one sense, the classroom is like the big game for the football player. The game is the significant moment. It completes the activity of all the hard practice; it is the real world.

Properly understood, the intellectual life informs the whole being of the person engaged in that life by affecting the spiritual, social, and moral activities of the person. In this tradition, one's ultimate purpose is not to gain information, but to gain a certain orientation, a certain formation. That orientation has to do with being open to reality and to the claims of reality. What this means is that the participant does not close himself off to examining his own opinions in the light of questions that challenge those opinions. His orientation permits him to go where truth will lead him. Out of this orientation comes a generosity manifested as the willingness of the person to give himself for the sake of truth, as did Socrates and Christ. It is an orientation that permits one to see the truth as friend and to be willing to give one's life for that friend. What this orientation means is that one is expected to be a lover of truth and a lover of those who engage in the love of truth. It is a kind of love that overflows one's own being and permits others to share in that love.

This orientation produces a freedom for the students. Through participation in liberal arts education, the student is freer than he has ever been and probably ever will be. In several senses he is free. He has stepped back from the day-to-day activity of societal life in order to discourse with the best minds. Distractions of job, of family, political involvement, and other involvements have been put aside to be picked up later. Never again will the student have the time to engage in leisurely activity as he has in a liberal arts undergraduate program. Hearing about this freedom might sound strange to a student who is caught up with class schedules, papers, and readings, but the freedom is still there.

*For an elaboration on this idea, see Pieper, Josef, *Leisure the Basis of Culture.* (Tr. by Alexander Dru.) N.Y.: Pantheon, 1952.

There is also a freedom that has to do with being free to roam over time and space in order to discourse with the best minds. This is quite a freedom since one is freed from the limitations of living in a certain time and place in seeking one's spiritual masters. One cannot love wisdom alone, as Plato points out by his use of the dialogue from in his philosophical writings. Truth emerges out of discourse. Discourse can only take place when several persons are engaged in the love of truth. When wonder informs the members of a community, it informs them in such a way that there is a desire for discourse. One will talk about what one is interested in. Another aspect, then, of freedom brought about by liberal arts is the freedom to engage in discourse.

The love that is spoken of in liberal arts is a real love. It is love of truth and love of delight that comes with the completion of wonder; and it is the love the participants have for each other. But when one loves something, there is risk involved. One becomes vulnerable in love to the slights that may come from the object of love, or from failing the object of love, or from slights that come from those with whom one loves. Suffering results from loving. If one is not attached to anything, if one does not love, no risk is involved, no vulnerability, and no suffering. Again, if we look at the life of Socrates, it is illuminating. It is Socrates who by virtue of his love permits himself to suffer and to die at the hands of his fellow Athenians. It is Callicles in the *Gorgias*, the opponent of Socrates, who will not permit himself to be put in a position of suffering. Rhetoric, according to Callicles, permits one to get out of being punished when one does wrong, or enables one to become a tyrant in order to avoid becoming the victim of a tyrant. But, if one loves, one must love like Socrates and accept the possibility of suffering for the sake of love and for the sake of those whom one loves. Liberal arts education, then, forms a person whose loyalty and destiny are interwoven with his concrete society.

In arguing for the fullness of the liberal arts tradition, I must disagree with Jefferson. In his "Report of the Commissioners for the University of Virginia" Jefferson details a curriculum rooted in ten areas, five mathematical and scientific and five based on language both modern and ancient, government, law, and what he calls ideology or doctrine of thought. Included in doctrine of thought are general grammar, ethics, rhetoric, *belles lettres*, and fine arts. There is no theology. Hence, there is a great loss of understanding.

Loss of faith results in loss of understanding. It is not a coincidence that the secularization process that occurred in Europe in the nineteenth and early twentieth centuries denied the unity of the human race by manufacturing racist ideologies. This same loss of faith was accompanied by the loss of the sacramental vision of nature, a vision which had recognized the full value of the created world. It was replaced with the secular view that nature was simply an instrument of man to be used to increase his power.

When faith is lost, liberal arts education too becomes distorted. It loses its own vision when its curriculum becomes fragmented and when it encourages sophistry, triviality, or ideology. Marx and Nietzsche, to take two examples of such a loss, were thoroughly educated in a deficient version of liberal arts, one no longer illuminated by faith. The terrible fragmentation that gave rise to and resulted from the ideologies of these two men is an indictment of this kind of education. The knowledge presented by faith--knowledge of community, creation, suffering, death, resurrection, and the person--when it is present in a liberal arts curriculum, does much to prevent the loss of a full human vision. The purpose of the liberal arts is to enable the students to know the nature of the order of being and the relationships within that order. By its knowledge of the transcendent dimension of being, faith casts light on all the order of being and reveals the great variety of partnerships in being. Thus, faith and the liberal arts are partners in knowing the order of being and in the articulation of that knowledge. Accordingly, I have to part company here with Jefferson and with my good friends who have structured their curriculum purely on the great books.

I also have to part company with my friends who think that philosophy alone can structure a liberal arts curriculum. What tends to be neglected in this approach is the imagination. This approach treats literature as if it were moral philosophy or recreation. It forgets that literature is itself a mode of knowledge and essential to all other modes of knowledge. One of the just criticisms levelled against the liberal education of the Fifties was this neglect of the imagination. This neglect was serious, for one of the major components of the West is the symbolic imagination expressed in literature. It is my opinion that not much work has been done on the dynamics of the imagination and, in particular, its relationship to the intelligence. In my work with students, I find that the most imaginative are the most intelligent. I suspect, then, a symbiotic relationship between the two but that is just an impression. The map of imagination has yet to come across my purview if it does exist.

It has been said that the Founding Fathers built better than they knew. In the sense that they thought and acted within a tradition which they did not create but inherited and which continued after them the statement is true. One can describe that tradition in many ways. One way of describing it is that America is a land of forgiveness, that one can get a fresh start here, that by dint of hard work and talents, one can get ahead. The virtue that we have to speak of is the virtue of hope, not in the theological but in the political sense. When Madison states that there are unequal and diverse talents and that the primary object of government is to protect inequality and diversity, ironically hope is generated that one has some control over his destiny. An enforced condition of equality would stifle hope. Jefferson's defense of the natural aristocracy has the same hopeful effect. It is this providing of hope that places the Founding Fathers in the American tradition.

There is a continual newness about America. One is struck when reading early American history by the number and significance of the symbol "new." John Winthrop, a Puritan, tells us "...that men shall say of succeeding plantations: 'The Lord make it like that of New England.' For we must consider that we shall be a city upon a hill, the eyes of all people are upon us." With the same Puritans there is the symbol of the New Jerusalem. The Founding Fathers saw America as the new Rome, republican, of course, not imperial. Of course, we are inhabitants of the New World and participants in the *novus ordo saeculorum*. One is entitled to say that the *homonoia* of our society is hope based on renewal. It is that virtue that holds us together. Whenever our leaders recognize this public virtue, they find a response in the people, Franklin D. Roosevelt and Ronald Reagan being the best examples of this. This *homonoia* is something that the left does not recognize and why it does not win national elections in America. This is what permits huge waves of immigrants to be Americanized fairly quickly. And it accounts for the large amounts of time and money volunteered by Americans to worthy causes. But this hope, whose origin is properly grounded in American history, has a tendency to slide off into utopian expectations. One has only to read the speeches of Woodrow Wilson to discover this tendency. It is liberal education in its fullness with its vision of the possibilities and limits of man that can serve as a corrective to this tendency and helps keep hope grounded in reality.

In conclusion, let me say that it may be argued that a commercial republic should require commerce to be its predominant mode of education for its citizens. But there is really no need for the commercial republic to so insist. Commerce will not let one forget about the demands of commerce. We will be formed by a commercial republic almost whether or not we wish it. It is the contemplative spirit that is easily forgotten about in the rush of daily affairs. It is that spirit for which time must be deliberately set aside. Without this deliberate effort a great man such as Madison will be hard to come by and good citizens as well. We would have had a far different, and, one may surmise, a bad constitution had not our James Madison been intimately familiar with much Greek and more Latin, with Aristotle and Thucydides, with Cicero and Plutarch, with Blackstone and Locke. That is to say, he received an education in the man and found it wonderfully practical for the citizen and the statesman. The best education, then, to accompany our free institutions is the education worthy of free men, that is to say, a liberal education.

THE HISTORICAL DEVELOPMENT AND PROGRESSIVE DECADENCE OF AMERICAN EDUCATION

by Richard H. Powers

Leaders of the Reformation in sixteenth-century Germany made the first systematic effort to develop a system of compulsory public education in the hope of developing new and better impulses in the young. They established schools to train children in the liberal arts and in Christian discipline, where they would be raised "to become responsible men and women who can govern churches, countries, households, children and servants." These Protestant leaders understood and foresaw every practical problem. They realized that their purpose could only be accomplished by a carefully trained cadre of teachers operating under the aegis of strong-willed governments. These teachers were compelled to swear to articles which prescribed teaching methods, curriculum, and texts. All schools had a uniform teaching program and list of books. Uniformity was mandated so that no able scholar would escape detection, and so none would arrive at the university unprepared. Identical books and teaching methods were prescribed in order to permit common examinations throughout the state, so that the talent of teachers and students could be evaluated "by comparing them." The brightest students were to be moved up from lower to higher schools, and stipends were provided for the talented poor. Compulsory attendance protected the most able young from short-sighted or ignorant parents. The purpose of all this was to ensure that the best minds be developed and their potential contribution not be lost.

The passage from lower to higher schools was determined by sensible discrimination:

> Because individuals are variously endowed with
> mental gifts and aptitudes teachers must make careful
> discrimination so that no sluggish mind is overtaxed,
> which would only lead to frustration and rebellion,
> and no intellect remain unchallenged, a sad waste of
> human resources.[1]

Modern national systems of universal and compulsory education were founded on similar principles. The presumption of an authoritarian cultural elite which defined both the purpose and content of education was always implicit.

The subordination of knowledge to political purposes today explains why so many stereotypes of historical experience are often deliberate deceptions. What is most repeated about our "democratic" heritage is frequently mendacious. James Madison, the "master builder" of our Constitution, believed that he had constructed a document which protected talent from the jealousy and resentment of the majority. He noted that the diversity in the faculties of men was an insuperable obstacle to a uniformity of interests. And, in his words, "the protection of these faculties is the first object of government."[2] All of this mirrors a view of things central in Western culture from Plato onwards. In Plato's ideal society differences in rank and responsibility would be determined solely by one's faculties. Everyone would perform functions for which his nature best fitted him, and no one assumed a role for which he or she was unfit. Guardians would oversee education which would prepare and train, and serve to identify and select, those worthy to be advanced from step to higher step until only the very best remained, those suited to rule. Translated into modern terms this became "equal opportunity." Public education, available to all, was to open careers to talent. Justice, as Plato had insisted, was presumed to require that every individual be placed in the function and station which capacity, with regard only to talent and virtue, entitled him.

Thomas Jefferson, the most democratic of our Founding Fathers, imagined a scheme of education of this very sort. Jefferson proposed public educational institutions so that "worth and genius" could be sought out "from every condition of life" by selection based on scholarly attainment in the earliest years. Three years of free education for all would be provided in local schools. Each year the most able child among those whose parents were too poor to give him or her further education would be selected from each local school to be sent to one of the twenty grammar schools established throughout Virginia by the state. At the end of two years at the grammar school "the best genius" among all the poor boys enrolled was to be selected to be supported another six years, the others to be dismissed. In time, every year twenty poor boys in the state, "raked from the rubbish," was Jefferson's term, would complete grammar school. Half of these would be eliminated, the superior ten sent to William and Mary at public expense to be educated for positions of leadership. The state was to prescribe the curriculum at every level, to mandate methods, and to establish a system of inspection to insure conformity, and protection against community efforts to alter standards.[3] Like Plato, like the Protestant leaders of the Reformation, Jefferson took for granted a self-confident ruling elite which would determine the purpose and content of education.

In the American colonies Latin grammar schools and colleges served the needs of a very few from backgrounds which had interest in such education and the means to afford it. Elementary schools and the apprentice system were designed for the poor. In general, religious groups were allowed to control their own schools while sharing in public funds. Very few children, however, ever attended school.[4]

Following the Declaration of Independence the states, almost at once, undertook to provide schools. By the time Ohio was admitted to the Union in 1803 the principle of state responsibility for education was incorporated in state constitutions as a matter of course. The common justification was sounded in the Ordinance of 1787 by which Congress established the government of the Northwest Territory:

> Religion, morality, and knowledge being necessary
> to the good government and happiness of mankind,
> schools and the means of education shall forever be
> encouraged.[5]

By 1833 every state had ended public support to church schools. This cleared the way for all of the states to establish a free common-school system. By 1870 public elementary schooling was universal and practically every white American over the age of ten could read and write. Ninety-five percent of the nation's nearly six million illiterates were either black people or white immigrants from Europe.[6] Free public secondary education was widely available, and some states had already capped their public system with universities. As late as 1876, however, only three or four percent of public school students went on to high school, and a large majority of those who attended college came from private academies.

Decentralization, and the huge growth of public elementary institutions and students, meant almost universal interference and dictation by local communities in the conduct of these schools. Elitist notions were not often dominant in American communities. Secondary schools, on the other hand, remained largely free from these pressures, mainly, it was explained, "because the people as such are not interested in education from which they do not profit." Demagogues often attacked the very existence of public high schools, complaining that most of the poor derived no benefit from them.[7]

In 1849 the president of Middlebury College, noting the scale of immigration, asked whether these adopted citizens might not prove "to our republic what the Goths and Huns were to the Roman Empire?" The answer, he feared, was in the hands of our elementary teachers.[8] Because the population of our country was so diverse and dispersed, badly needing education in the rudiments as well as a sense of national culture, Horace Mann argued for the school as a common social institution. Given the diverse and dispersed control of the elementary school system what was to be common was quickly in dispute. Even within Massachusetts itself one of Mann's colleagues warned that if the passion for expanding the curriculum continued "every county in the state will need an insane hospital."[9] Such problems did not become crucial for secondary schools until nearly the end of the century. Of concern to only a few, who shared or accepted traditional views, secondary and college education were based on the same assumptions. The classics, mathematics, history, and philosophy were accepted as the essential content of liberal education.

The older public secondary education in the United States was conservative, in that it accepted the existing order of society and called upon the child to assert himself within its framework. Only a small minority of children attended, but it was democratic in that it assumed that there were children from every class of society who were capable, by native endowment, to enter with some degree of hope into the world of academic competition--the mastery of subject matter, and discipline of mind and character. Children were judged by educational standards, and those standards were not subject to re-definition to suit the capabilities of the average child. Then the United States began to develop free public secondary education on a large scale, and was one of the first nations to make secondary school attendance compulsory, first in Massachusetts, in 1852. By 1890 twenty-seven states required it, by 1918 every state.[10]

A huge expansion in the number of students brought a new clientele into confrontation with the traditional high-school curriculum. Pressure quickly developed to be "responsive" to the needs of those who would not later attend college, and to satisfy the demand for "practical" instruction. The confusion led the National Education Association to establish a Committee of Ten to standardize the high school curriculum. In 1892, headed by Charles W. Eliot, president of Harvard, the committee found that there were some forty subjects taught somewhere nationwide, but that thirteen of these were offered at very few schools. The basic curriculum was limited to twenty-seven subjects. Self-assured guardians of traditional wisdom and practice, members of the committee, although they recognized that the secondary school was a terminal rather than a college preparatory institution for most of its students, recommended that the same subjects, taught in the same manner, be offered to both groups. A set of four alternative courses was recommended, but all required four years of English, four years of foreign language, and three years each of history, mathematics, and science.[11]

114

Eliot and his colleagues represented an authority whose prestige was waning, and would soon be eclipsed. Dominion in secondary education passed from those with a traditional understanding of what education should be to those who defined it in terms more attuned to a populist era. The period between 1890 and 1914 was a time of mass immigration of non-English speaking, illiterate people. By 1911 more than 50 percent of the public school population of our thirty-seven largest cities was first generation American.[12] During World War I the mass influx of subliterate blacks from the South to the industrial North began. And between 1890 and 1914 the percentage of all adolescents entering high school rose from 10 to 40 percent.[13] President Eliot had declared that the "policy of an institution of education, of whatever grade, ought never be determined by the needs of the least capable students."[14] This philosophy would have been difficult to maintain in the conditions which developed in the United States. The difficulty was not faced.

By the end of World War I our secondary schools were dominated by an increasing number of pupils who were not only unselected but who were also unwilling, a captive audience, in school because the law forced them to go. As the twentieth century progressed high schools were filled with a growing proportion of doubtful, reluctant, unsuited, and actually hostile pupils. Instead of regarding these students as obstacles, or as special problems in a school system devoted to educating the interested and capable, American educators exploited public credulity and entered upon a crusade to exalt the academically uninterested and ungifted child. These professionals won influence in our educational system by justifying the hostility of the mediocre to the old ideal of education by proclaiming it to be archaic and futile, and by preaching that "a truly democratic" system was one which met the child's immediate interests by offering a series of "practical and useful" things.

The crucial question was the academic curriculum. Statistics reveal the melancholy victory of those who pretended that academic subjects were irrelevant for the mass of secondary school students. Latin, taken by 49 percent of all students in 1911, was taken by 8 percent in 1949. Modern language enrollment fell from 84 to 22 percent, mathematics enrollment from 90 to 55 percent. In 1911 more pupils were studying a foreign language, or mathematics, or history, or English--any of these--than all non-academic subjects combined. By 1941 some 274 subjects were offered in high schools.[15] But in 1941 the changes had little effect on the college bound, who still enrolled in academic subjects. The most violent stages of the revolution were still to come.

Shortly after World War II the United States Commissioner of Education announced that only seven out of ten youths were entering high school, and that only four of these graduated, in spite of forty years of trying to increase the "holding power" of schools. "Enriching" the curriculum tenfold had failed to accomplish its purpose. The Commissioner concluded that the curriculum had not been enriched enough. He and his colleagues declared that 80 percent of the nation's youth were unfit for academic studies. The solution proposed, and widely followed, was to have secondary schools engage primarily in "life adjustment" education.[16] Twenty years later the percentage of youth who graduated from high school had nearly doubled; what a graduate had to know halved.

In our society the public school, at every level, is necessarily in harmony with majority standards. Every innovative educational practice of the last half century has appealed to widespread resentment and rebelliousness against the discipline that excellence demands, against recognition of natural and inevitable qualitative differences in individual human beings. Our system simply accommodates community standards. In recent years SAT scores have been a measure of the resulting decline in secondary education. Today one-third of all high school graduates take the tests each year, two-thirds of the freshman class in colleges and universities. The test taking group is made up of our best students. The decline in performance which the scores reflect, great as it has been, is much less than the decline they do not measure--that in the skills of the majority of students who do not take them.

The highest national average achieved by students taking the tests was in 1963, after which it dropped annually for two decades. In 1963, when the score was highest, 478, it was not high enough to gain entrance to better private colleges and universities, was well below the score such institutions thought necessary in order to profit from higher education. Today a majority of college freshmen have a lower score.

In colonial times there were nine colleges in America. By 1876 there were 545 colleges and universities in the United States. The number prompted the artless comment that "the means of instruction is far greater than those capable of profiting from it." Today over three thousand colleges and universities exist. The number of students tripled between 1920 and 1940, and quadrupled again by 1980. It took some time before explicitly egalitarian theories, which were the grounds for denaturing secondary education, began to have a decisive influence on higher education, but a combination of ostensibly different forces had similar consequences.

For many centuries following their founding in the Middle Ages universities were conservative institutions. Their traditional purpose was to educate a minority, selected on the basis of the promise demonstrated in its earlier schooling. Their purpose was to prepare an elite, whose personal temperament and intellectual ability qualified it for responsibility and leadership. A religion and philosophy prevailed which was taken to be the expression of ultimate and immutable truth, wisdom, and morality. Therefore, intellectual and moral education could be imparted, once and for all, in the early years of life. In the course of a long period during which higher education remained traditional there were additions to the body of

116

knowledge, but no institutions were so little affected by the dynamic intellectual, technological, and scientific developments of the sixteenth, seventeenth, and eighteenth centuries as were universities. In the second half of the nineteenth century, however, the vast expansion of knowledge, the spread of liberal ideology, and representative institutions, brought real change.

Dante, it is said, knew practically everything there was to be known in Western Christendom in the 1350. Goethe knew the greater part of what there was to be known in 1800. Not much more than a generation later it became impossible for the most powerful intellect to master more than a fraction of what there was to be known. The accelerating pace of change in science and technology and institutions created circumstances in which the university student was required to specialize in order to acquire knowledge with sufficient thoroughness to enable him to use it in professional life. This specialization had a high price. As the twentieth century progressed the most educated, in the formal sense, came to suffer as much as did the uneducated from parochialism and ignorance. Once the central purpose of higher education, intellectual and moral education declined until it became vestigial, and, finally, at most institutions, insignificant.

The "explosion" of knowledge forced modification of higher learning. But knowledge, not wisdom, "exploded." What Dante or Goethe could tell us about science or technology would now be useless. Either, most certainly, speak to us with more wisdom than we are in the habit of hearing about the most difficult and complex problems of our everyday lives. Every man and woman, in our time or in any time, ought to know as much as their powers of comprehension permit of what Dante and Goethe knew. Ultimate and immutable truth, as they relate to wisdom and morality, are limited and static, at least in the sense that no "education" can ever hope to raise many to the level of understanding which the greatest minds have achieved in the past. Education, in this fundamental aspect, remains essentially static. Today the university's primary function, the teaching and transmission of higher culture, has been abandoned to the point where the vast majority of our students pass through institutions of higher learning without being touched by it. Until the 1960's, specialization and professionalism, not democratic or egalitarian ideology, was the excuse, but this abandonment has been a matter of lament for nearly a century now. No complaint was ever more futile.

Freud noted that in viewing a civilization

> one gets the impression that culture is something which is imposed on a resisting majority by a minority that understands how to possess itself of the means of power and coercion.[17]

Henry Adams wrote in 1870 that the political dilemma in the United States was as clear at that moment as it was likely to be in 1970. The system of 1789 had broken down, and with it the eighteenth century fabric of *a priori* or moral principles. The system was, or soon would be, the poorest in the world.[18] It is academic custom to denigrate such pessimism. But the plight of American education is not rooted in peculiar causes. It suffers from a common malady.

John Stuart Mill, although he welcomed the growth of democratic institutions, feared that with their growth in the future the stupid majority might coerce the wise minority. He so much trusted reason that he believed that his essay "On Liberty" might serve to help prevent the majority from following its natural inclination to intolerance. A member of an elite which did not doubt its own premises, Mill's educational proposals were as authoritarian as those of the Christian leaders of Reformation Germany. Neither teachers nor students were part of his decision-making process. He understood the overwhelming difficulty. He and his kind were too few. He complained that, "if given absolute power tomorrow" to impose his educational program on the country, he would fail from the impossibility of finding "fit instruments" to carry out the teaching.[19]

In 1905 Henry James spoke of American literary production, "untouched by criticism, unguided, unlighted, uninstructed, unashamed." He observed,

> the biggest flock straying without shepherds...without a sound of the sheepdog's bark..that ever found room for pasture. The very opposite has happened from what might have been expected...The shepherds have diminished as the flock has increased--quite as if number and quantity had got beyond them, or even as if their charge had turned, by some uncanny process, to a pack of ravening wolves.[20]

More than a quarter of a century before James made this comment about literature Harvard had inaugurated an elective system from which students could select at pleasure their own program of studies. Henry Cabot Lodge remarked that under the previous compulsory plan

> a certain amount of knowledge, no more useless than any other, and a still larger discipline of learning, were forced on all alike. Under the new system it is possible to escape without learning anything at all, by a judicious selection of unrelated subjects taken up only because they were easy or because the burden imposed by those who taught them was light.[21]

Even Harvard students had become "a flock straying without shepherds." President Eliot had introduced this system. He must have been disappointed, Irving Babbit thought, to see how nearly all Harvard students flocked

> into a few large classes; and especially disappointed
> that many of them should take advantage of the
> elective system...to lounge through their college
> course along the line of least resistance. [22]

Before World War I Babbit found that specialization at Harvard had already gone so far that even faculty members had no common culture, hardly two were to be found who had read the same book.[23] He declared that any discussion of the place of literature in the college was conditioned, already, by the previous question: "whether there will be any college for literature to have a place in."[24] So long ago, and in so select an institution, Babbit spoke of colleagues "in whom the delicate balance between sympathy and judgment had been lost," who were ready to lower the standard of an institution rather than inflict an apparent hardship on an individual, of humanitarians who saw college not so much as the means for the thorough training of the few as for the uplift of the many.[25] But in 1908 Babbit was singular only in his candid observations about the reality within colleges, not in his educational values. Those values, in so far as higher education was concerned, were loudly professed by almost everyone who ought to have mattered.

In 1917, for example, a conference was held at Princeton University on the value of the classics. For the occasion some three hundred statements in support of the primacy of the classics in higher education were collected. The presidents of thirty-five of our most prestigious colleges and universities, and the heads of practically every well-known college preparatory school or academy, protested against specialization and utilitarian schemes of education which were having the consequence of relegating Greek and Latin to the category of electives. Three former presidents of the United States, the incumbent president, and a future president, three past Secretaries of State, three former presidents of the American Bar Association, and some two dozen presidents of railroads, great banks, and insurance, manufacturing and publishing firms joined the chorus. Former President Theodore Roosevelt insisted that the most traditional educational theories and values were not only applicable to a democracy but ought to have a special force in our country. He wrote:

> Democracy comes short of what it should be just to
> the extent that it fails to provide for the exceptional
> individual, no matter how poor his start in life, the
> highest kind of exceptional training; for democracy as
> a permanent world force must mean not only raising
> the general level but also raising the standard of
> excellence to which only exceptional individuals may
> attain. [26]

119

Roosevelt did not think that the "average boy," or even the average college student was suited to a thorough liberal education based on the classics. But certain institutions, he believed, must satisfy the needs of the best. For these students he prescribed Greek or Latin, and if possible both of these two classical languages and literatures, one modern foreign language, and a wide sweep of general history, science, philosophy, and modern literature. Every man destined for leadership in the professions, in business, or in politics should have all of this. Roosevelt understood the diversity among institutions and among their students. He proposed only that some few provide for these few students, the very best, whose needs most colleges and universities would never be able to meet. When he wrote none required the program he outlined, no institution was doing what he declared certain institutions must do. Nevertheless, although the degradation of democratic dogma was already leading to the defeat of such notions in secondary education, meritocracy and elitism remained the fundamental premises in public discussion of higher education.

Thirty years later President Truman's Commission on Higher Education was appointed, at least in part, out of a traditional concern for the talented young. An anxiety, hardly conceivable in the politics of the future, that too many of the dull and too few of the brightest were attending college, was a motive for the Commission's existence. It recommended a score of 100 on the ACE Psychological Test as the threshold for entering college.[27] This threshold, to be sure, was significantly below that ordinarily achieved by all who entered better private institutions, was lower than that required to become a commissioned officer in the armed forces. On the other hand the mean entering score of entering freshmen at all colleges was below 100 at the time. The average college freshman had a lower score than that recommended, although the recommended score was not high enough to qualify for better institutions. Intelligence at the mean, or above mean level *was* declared to be a proper test for identifying those suited for higher education.

In the late 1950's a huge increase in the number and proportion of students enrolled in colleges and universities took place, students whose preparation, natural abilities, and attitudes paralleled those who had flooded into the high schools in the 1920's. In the 1950's half the students who entered four-year institutions of higher learning finished. By 1970 two-thirds of those who entered did not finish, in spite of a marked lowering of standards almost everywhere. Beginning in the mid 1960's colleges reduced the number and jazzed up the content of basic courses, weakened graduation requirements, and added a host of academically less demanding electives. Students were able to get through college more easily, with less preparation and higher grades, than ever before. Less qualified when they entered, less was done than ever before to correct their deficiencies. That even under these conditions two-thirds of the new type of college student dropped out before finishing a four-year program was used to justify the destruction of the higher education curriculum. The ideology long ascendant in leading schools of education, within major foundations, and always supreme within the federal educational bureaucracy, now succeeded in undermining the rational and intellectual foundations of higher education.

In 1956 Walter Whyte noted that the anti-intellectual sector of the educational establishment had usurped the word "democratic" to justify the denaturing of the high school and college curriculum. Once the uneducated had had the humility of ignorance. Now they were being given degrees and put in charge. The delusion of learning on their part, he believed, would produce disastrous consequences. By 1985, he predicted, not only would those who controlled the educational establishment be themselves the product of stringently anti-intellectual training, but laymen, equally the product of the social adjustment type of schooling, would have no other standard to evaluate the education of their own children.[28] It happened long before he expected.

By 1970 public concern, in so far as it was reflected by the federal government, was not whether too many dull or too few bright were enrolled in higher education, but that too many who began failed to finish their studies. According to an old adage of educationists, "nothing learned, nothing taught," the drop-out rate in the colleges proved that these institutions were at fault. In 1971 Frank Newman headed a committee which prepared a report on higher education for the Secretary of Health, Education and Welfare. The authors declared:

> It is not enough to improve and expand the present system...The system resists fundamental change, rarely eliminates outmoded programs...ignores the differing needs of students...and almost never creates different types of institutions.

When this statement was issued colleges and universities had already turned themselves inside out in the name of meeting the "needs" of students. Variation in the United States has been so great that a college degree, in itself, tells us nothing about what the holder knows or can do. Most seniors at some high schools are better educated, in the formal sense of having broader knowledge of our culture as well as superior language and mathematical skills, than are most graduates at some of our colleges.[29]

The Newman Report proposed that more alternative institutions be created, where students would not be expected to learn in the same way as at Harvard, institutions which would allow students to learn "in other ways than sitting in classrooms and reading books," and from which, it was implied, they would not drop out until they had finished. This would provide "access" for the "poor" and for minorities, and allow the Harvards to serve the intellectual elite. This was a demand for unconditional surrender. A large majority of our colleges were already alternatives to

121

anything which could possibly be described as elitist or archaic in curriculum or standards. For a long time there had been institutions geared to students of the lowest levels of academic competence, and these institutions had been increasing in number and size at a rate to provide places for any and all who desired a college degree.

It may be said that there has been a reaction against such views. In fact the views and policies of egalitarian educators are not likely to be defeated or overturned. Existing institutions have survived by adapting to their environment. Curriculum and admission policies are not determined by abstract principles. Admission policy must be adjusted to ensure enough students to fill classrooms. The curriculum must be tailored to ensure that these students are retained. The prevailing educational ideology is a rationalization which justifies a policy of primitive self-interest--the need to survive. Today federal loans, grants, and other aid pays about one-third of all college tuition, room and board bills. If subsidy for higher education were to be limited to those who demonstrate talent and academic promise, who attend rigorous institutions, and pursue useful programs, the resulting crisis within the college and university community would be similar to that which many of our farmers face when threatened with any serious modification of the price support system.

The defenders of traditional culture have, over many years, repeatedly described the plight of higher learning. The remedy which almost all have proposed is a return to a structured liberal arts curriculum. Generation after generation has seen a further erosion of that curriculum. Traditionalists have grown weaker and weaker within the academic community, their influence less and less. They have never been weaker on college and university faculties than today, and will be weaker tomorrow. Outside assistance is their only hope.

At the elementary and secondary level the public classroom cannot rise far above the contemporary standards of our egalitarian society. At the college and university level this might, under certain circumstances, be less true. But more recent developments should not obscure the awful truth. The minority Freud mentions lost control of higher education long ago. Irving Babbit explained that, for this very reason, liberal education was in difficulty in this country before any of us were born. For this reason, a half-century ago, Robert Hutchins declared that the chief characteristic of the higher learning in America was disorder.

In 1936 Hutchins published a book in which he pleaded that some institutions, at least, demonstrate what the higher learning was. The talented poor, he believed, should be granted free education through college. Every reason for doing this, however, would be debased if those granted this opportunity were permitted "to wander at will through the higher learning." Authority should dictate the content of higher education. Otherwise, Hutchins wrote, "university degrees cease to have any meaning, indeed, cease to exist."[30] There could not be a university unless students and professors, "and particularly professors," had a common intellectual training.[31] He declared that a man certainly could not be called educated who had never read any of the great books of the Western world. Nevertheless, it was possible for a student to graduate from the finest American colleges without having read any of them.[32] Hutchins proposed a curriculum which would do all the things that the elective system did not. Were there fit instruments? No. He had to admit that no college or university faculty would approve his program. They would not have read the books they would have to teach.[33]

In 1962 Hutchins wrote a preface to a new edition of his book. In the midst of brutal victories over what remained of liberal education, he announced defeat. The trend toward vocationalism and triviality seemed to him irreversible. The time had come to forget about most of our existing institutions, and to plan new ones "that would undertake the overwhelmingly important task that existing colleges and universities had given up," the training of men and women to give intellectual leadership to their fellow citizens.[34]

For the better part of a century the majority of a college or university faculty almost everywhere stood ready to defeat any effort to impose a traditional liberal arts curriculum. Circumstances had long dictated that the only way to install this curriculum would have been for some authority to order faculties to stop doing what they were doing, and to do what they were told to do against their will. Now professors may hold diverse views about curriculum. Almost as one they believe in the right of the faculty to determine the curriculum, and its duty to defend this prerogative from any interference by the "administration," or, God forbid, the trustees. To propose outside coercion was utterly at odds with academic, and public, notions of legitimacy with regard to decision making, and Hutchins did not suggest it. He simply concluded that, because faculties could not be reformed, existing institutions were hopeless. He proposed new ones.

The difficulty Hutchins thought insuperable was certainly no greater than that facing the effort to start up new institutions of the proper kind. If reform was impossible his alternative was impossible. The requirements for either are much the same--wise shepherds, or shepherds influenced by wise men. What is possible?

We were treated several years ago to an outpouring of dismay and disbelief at the very remote possibility that those who control the most influential source of information in our country be divested of their monopoly. And at the risk of bringing terrible opprobrium upon myself I offer the example of Jesse Helms, in this sense: he understands what must be done, and the only way it can be done, to end a pervasive evil. He went to Ted Turner, who if converted, could help.* There is, indeed, no way that the defenders of traditional culture can sensibly aspire to power and influence in the academic world compared to that of CBS in its field of satisfying mass tastes for a profit. But if the defenders of traditional culture are endowed with some ability to explain and convince, these competencies ought to be applied where they can do some good. Their proper exercise is not on street corners, nor faculty meetings, not even on talk shows.

Public colleges and universities are not likely to be salvaged, nor is public support forthcoming for the type of institution Hutchins wished to see created. In theory, at least, existing private institutions need not be regarded as hopeless, even when their faculties, on the issue of the curriculum, are hopeless. Trustees appoint presidents of colleges and universities, they are the final authority which approves the appointment of deans, of faculty members, and the granting of tenure, the final authority in approving admission policy, degree requirements, programs, even courses. In public institutions trustees are named by governors, who are subject to the necessity of pleasing the prevailing factions which compose majority opinion. We do not see governors elected who regard themselves as guardians of higher culture and determined to impose it, nor can we expect them in the future. The trustees of private institutions are not selected by politicians. And, although their actions rarely reflect it, their personal convictions are not often in harmony with actual academic practices. As a group they are much more in need of greater confidence in the correctness and relevance of their convictions than of conversion. And there are a great many private institutions which might be significantly improved by an enlightened and self-assured board of trustees, and hardly any which might not be somewhat mended.

Strong-minded and stouthearted trustees would have to be in order to defy the abusive insubordination of their own faculty, and the indignation of the academic community at large. If they had enough success to find imitators the onslaught of the Dan Rathers and the Tom Wickers, possibly even that of Phil Donahue, would certainly follow. Nonetheless the traditionalist with the ambition to work some improvement in at least one institution of higher learning could do few things so practical as concentrating all effort on influencing its trustees. To Plato the drifting apart of men of thought and men of action was a disastrous calamity. The human race would never see the end of trouble until this changed. Within higher education those who presume themselves wise might strive, at least, to communicate with those "men of action" who have the responsibility and the power to decide what is done and is not done within colleges and universities.

*Editor's Note: Helms sought to convince enough people who saw CBS's news reporting as demonstrating a liberal bias to buy stock in the company so they could gain control and stop the bias.

For example, presume that a board of trustees is searching for a president. The effort might be made to convince the board that it ought to appoint a person who would promise to establish a four year sequence in the reading of great books, and a three-year foreign language requirement, for the B.A. degree; and who would take an oath to eliminate existing courses in pottery, the food gathering habits of primitive peoples, contemporary popular culture, and all programs designed to placate or pamper parochial interests or to encourage the self-importance of small groups, and to veto proposals for new ones. In any case, it is along these lines that, here and there, something good might be done.

NOTES

1. Powers, Richard H., *The Dilemma of Education in a Democracy.* Chicago: Regnery Gateway, 1984, pp. 132-35.

2. Hamilton, Alexander; Madison, James; and Jay, John, *The Federalist.* Cambridge: Harvard University Press, 1966, pp. 130-31.

3. Honeywell, Roy J., *The Educational Works of Thomas Jefferson.* Cambridge: Harvard University Press, 1931, pp. 199-205; Pippa, A. Alexander , *Educational Ideas in America.* New York: David McKay, 1969, pp. 130-32, 140.

4. Butts, Freeman R. and Cremin, Lawrence A., *A History of Education in American Culture.* New York: Holt, Rinehart & Winston, 1953, pp. 99, 236.

5. *Ibid.*, p. 245, and Knight, Edgar W. and Hall, Clifton L., *Readings in American Educational History.* New York: Appleton-Century-Crofts, 1951, p. 116.

6. Janet, Claudio, *Les Etats-Unis Contemprains.* Paris: E. Plon, 1876, p. 378.

7. *Ibid*, pp. 397-402.

8. Butts, pp. 191-92.

9. *Ibid.*, p. 218.

10. Knight, p. 297.

11. Gutek, Gerald L., *A History of the Western Educational Experience.* New York: Random House, 1972, p. 370; Butts, p. 390.

12. Hofstadter, Richard, *Anti-intellectualism in American Life.* New York: Alfred A. Knopf, 1963, p. 337.

13. *Ibid.*, pp. 326-27; Butts, p. 418; Hacker, Andrew, ed., *U/S A Statistical Portrait of the American People.* New York: Viking Press, 1983, p. 233.

14. Hofstadter, p. 365.

15. *Ibid.*, p. 341.

16. Krug, Edward A., *Salient Dates in American Education* : 1635-1964. New York: Harper & Row, 1966, pp. 131-35.

17. Freud, Sigmund, *The Future of an Illusion.* New York: W.W. Norton & Company, 1957, pp. 4-6.

18. Adams, Henry , *The Education of Henry Adams.* New York: The Library of America, 1983, p. 976.

19. Hayek, F.A., *John Stuart Mill and Harriet Taylor: Their Friendship and Subsequent Marriage.* New York: Augustus M. Kelley, 1970, p. 145.

20. James, Henry, *French Writers.* New York: The Library of America, 1984, p. 116.

21. Beard, Charles A. and Beard, Mary R., *America in Midpassage.* New York: Macmillan, 1939, p. 471.

22. Babbit,Irving, *Literature and the American College.* Boston: Houghton Mifflin, 1908, pp. 52-53.

23. *Ibid.*, p. 95.

24. *Ibid.*, p. 5.

25. *Ibid.*, p. 78.

26. West, Andrew F., ed., *Value of the Classics.* Princeton, N.J.: Princeton University Press, 1917, pp. 134-35.

27. Sanford, Nevitt, ed., *The American College: A Psychological and Social Interpretation of the Higher Learning.* New York: John Wiley & Sons, 1962, pp. 229-230.

28. Whyte, Walter H., Jr., *The Organization Man.* New York: Doubleday & Company, 1957, p. 110.

29. Sanford, pp. 227, 232.

30. Hutchins, Robert Maynard, *The Higher Learning in America.* New Haven: Yale University Press, 1936 (1962 ed.), p. 18.

31. *Ibid.*, p. 59.

32. *Ibid.*, p. 78.

33. *Ibid.*, p. 86.

34. *Ibid.*, p. xii.

RETROSPECTIVE REFLECTIONS ON *A NATION AT RISK*

by Annette Kirk

"Virtue or morality is a necessary spring of popular government."

--Washington's Farewell Address

During the past several years this nation has gone through educational ferment, debate, legislative action, soul-searching about education--all this since the report of the National Commission on Excellence in Education was issued in April, 1983. More than thirty other national reports on education followed the publication of *A Nation at Risk*, and almost three hundred reports from state commissions and task forces.

More than one million copies of the Commission's report have been distributed. There has occurred an intense and overwhelming response from the mass media, as well as from learned societies and scholarly journals.

The chief contribution of the federal government, under the Reagan Administration, was the publicizing and encouraging of state and local initiatives. The Administration sponsored twelve regional forums to disseminate and discuss the Report's recommendations; and it held a national forum late in 1983 at Indianapolis--the largest educational gathering ever convened--of people who ordinarily gathered only in their own professional or educational groups.

Public officials, professors, parents, teachers, school-board members, and even union representatives and persons interested in home schooling or religious schools came together for three days to dispute or to agree about all aspects of American education, and to respond to *A Nation at Risk*. Such an extensive follow-up to a public report never before had been undertaken.

In May, 1984, President Reagan announced the Academic Fitness Awards and new school-recognition awards. In various other ways, the Reagan Administration sustained the movement toward educational reform and provided leadership.

It has been at the level of state governments, however, that most initiatives for reform have begun. Proposals for such changes have been made in all fifty states. Meanwhile, the private sector, including professional associations, foundations, and businesses, has made impressive contributions. Perhaps no school in the country has been altogether unaffected by the wave of reform.

Why did this Report make such an impact? First, because the country was ready for such a study: the public was in a mood to receive its findings and accept its recommendations. Second, the Report was a readable, jargon-free document, pithy and to the point.

The Report reminded parents that they are the first educators of their children, and that they have the right and the responsibility to participate in their children's schooling. It told them that they must help their children understand how excellence cannot be achieved without intellectual and moral integrity, coupled with hard work and commitment; that both parents and teachers must be models of these virtues. As a result of the report and the other reports which followed it, the stage was set for a national debate on the strengths and weaknesses of American education.

Since the release of the report, some progress has been made--notably in the establishing of standards for graduation from high school. Experiments are underway in teacher training, the length of the school year, and the academic qualifications of athletes. Improvement has also been made in the interruption of classes for non-academic purposes, the grading system, and many other areas depending on the school district or state.

The Report concluded that the decline in educational standards and expectations was caused by "weakness of purpose and confusion of vision." It suggested that we may lose our shared vision of America and the spiritual fabric of our society unless we renew the one and repair the other.

We are now in the midst of an even hotter debate than the one concerned with specific school reforms. We are now discussing whether and to what extent religious knowledge and practice will be included in textbooks, curriculum, and school life. The debate has forced parents and educators to acknowledge the failure of schools to teach "values" divorced from moral norms. It seems time to return to teaching the "old bag of virtues," so disdainfully tossed out by Sixties social scientists. Such considerations become increasingly urgent as revelations of corruption in our city school systems both shock and depress us.

A subcommittee of the Commission briefly considered this subject of moral education. The members mused about the possibility of employing the Tao of C.S. Lewis (in *The Abolition of Man*) as a starting point for this discussion. The Tao is a list of convictions held by all of the major religions and religious philosophies. It includes respect for ancestors or elders, honesty in one's dealings with others, principles of mercy and justice, and other great ethical insights. This subcommittee did not continue to meet because of the press of time and preoccupation with academic aspects of schooling.

Nevertheless, before long there must be achieved some consensus as to what normative beliefs and behavior children are expected to learn so that they may live moral lives in community. Just now we are living on the moral capital of our parents' and grandparents' convictions. Every generation must make such beliefs their own, or else soon these norms will sound hollow. Into such a vacuum we have now fallen, and so our young are gravely confused.

In *The Emperor's New Clothes*, William Kirk Kilpatrick tells us that "Moral development is not simply a matter of becoming more rational or acquiring decision-making skills. It has to do with vision, the way one looks at life...It follows that one of the central tasks of moral education is to nourish the imagination with rich and powerful images of the kind found in stories, myths, poems, biography and drama. If we wish our children to grow up with a deep and adequate vision of life, we must provide a rich fund for them to draw on."

It was this Commission member's concern that literature once again should serve to nurture a moral imagination which led to the Report's recommendation that "The study of literature should...enhance imagination and ethical understanding." I believe much more attention must be given to this aspect of schooling.

As we continue to argue about how to implement administrative and academic reform, we must also resolve how to repair our shared vision and spiritual fabric. For although we now have computers to gather information and to catalogue and correlate it, computers cannot meditate and make moral decisions. We need persons who are able to integrate information, who are knowledgeable and reflective; persons who take long views, who possess a sense of history. The real risk to the nation is that our children will not have been reared in schools that pass on our moral patrimony.

"Where is the wisdom we have lost in knowledge? Where is the knowledge we have lost in information?"

--T.S. Eliot

ELEMENTARY AND SECONDARY SCHOOL REFORM: WHY IT FAILED

by Lawrence A. Uzzell

I have been involved with the Intercollegiate Studies Institute, the organization which sponsored the symposium from which most of the papers in this book are derived, for more than half its history, and this is the first time to my knowledge it focused part of a symposium program strictly on elementary-secondary education. Both cultural and political conservatives have tended to concentrate on higher education, not elementary-secondary education. I grant there is a sound organizational reason for this: ISI is an organization of people in higher education, and the defects of the colleges and universities are highly visible to most of us.

But I would suggest that we should pay more attention than we have to elementary-secondary education, for two reasons: First, the decadence of higher education is in part a product of the decadence of lower education-- colleges have to spend substantial time and energy teaching things their students should have learned in junior high school. Second, and this is more important for those of us who are directly involved in public policy, I would argue that for the most part the failings of today's colleges and universities were not caused by the government and are not going to be corrected by the government. Much as I would like to, I cannot blame the Department of Education for the fact that it is now possible for an undergraduate at Yale to fulfill his distributional requirements by taking courses on the history of rock and roll.

I would contrast that with the problems of elementary-secondary

131

education. The *primary* causes of these problems are mostly bad government policies. It is the government that has drained decision-making power from local school boards; it is the government that protects disruptive students from punishment; it is the government that forces schools to hire education majors in preference to liberal arts graduates. Now, the easiest way to correct dishonest and stupid government policies is clearly through honest and intelligent government policies. Thus I would suggest that those of us who seek education reform through the vehicles of government and politics should devote most of our attention to elementary and secondary education.

I would also suggest that this is why there was such a spirit of optimism in the mid-1980's about elementary-secondary reform. People sensed that their political leaders had finally come to see that the schools were in scandalously poor shape, and that they were finally willing to do something about it.

It is now clear this optimism was largely misplaced. It was misplaced because the reform movement was and still is essentially defined and controlled by the very institutions that are in need of reform. To an extraordinary degree, it is the public school establishment that has organized the conferences, written the reports, and drafted the legislation. It is as if we had entrusted the job of reforming defense contracting to the military-industrial complex, or the job of deregulating transportation to the Teamsters Union. Thus it is not surprising that the current reform movement has not really challenged the core cultural and ideological assumptions that have governed the schools for most of the twentieth century. Let me talk about four of these assumptions:

First, the current reform movement assumes that the purpose of education is entirely materialistic. In this book, we often see words like "character," "wisdom," "virtue," "right reason." But these words are not all that easy to find in the works of the recent commissions and task forces on educational excellence. They prefer words like "productivity," "security," and "economic growth"--as if the only reason for learning were to compete with the Japanese. In recent years, sensing that parents are increasingly dissatisfied with the moral vacuum in public education, reformers have begun to talk about "values." But a closer look at the curricula they recommend shows that by "values" they mean the skills and attitudes needed to be successful careerists and loyal citizens--not the higher virtues of the hero, philosopher or saint.

Second, the current reform movement assumes that the task of schooling is merely to develop "skills." It assumes that as long as you learn *how* to read, it doesn't matter what you read, be it Samuel Johnson or Robert Heinlein. Not long ago I happened to be in a bookstore near a suburban high school, and I saw a shelf full of copies of the Cliff's Notes for the collected works of Robert Heinlein. In 1901 the College Board published a list of specific book titles which it said every college freshman should have read. Today's College Board would not dare publish such a list, because too many of its constituents no longer believe that there is any core of knowledge or of civilization that ought to be passed on to every educated person. They act as if we should be satisfied with high-school graduates who get high SAT scores but who have never heard of Homer or Moses or the Federalist Papers. The schools based on this philosophy are producing what one friend of mine calls "techno-peasants"; a society based on this philosophy may be materially prosperous, but it will be impoverished in every other way.

Third, the current reform movement assumes that education is value-free. In the face of campaigns by every subculture from the feminists to the fundamentalists, trying to tilt the curriculum in their own favor, the current reform movement persists in the belief that it is possible to find a lowest common denominator that is equally inoffensive to everybody. In fact, this is not only not possible: it's not even *desirable.* The mere attempt has given us the blandest, most lifeless, most boring generation of textbooks in the history of formal education. One year, the educational think tank I previously headed hired a young historian to examine twenty of the most widely used high-school history textbooks, to find out how they treat religion as an historical phenomenon. He concluded that if a child's only source of information were these books, that child would believe that after the year 1700 religion was completely without importance in American life and American culture. These books treat religion the way the Victorians treated sex: it's a topic to be avoided whenever possible. That view is of course unacceptable not only to any serious Christian or Jew, but to anyone who believes that one of the marks of an educated man is that he knows how his ancestors were different from himself. Our study, authored by Dr. Robert Bryan, has since been confirmed by other scholars such as Professor Paul Vitz at New York University. Many educators at least now acknowledge the problem--but the public schools have yet to offer a plausible solution.

Fourth, the current reform movement assumes that the key to education reform is more centralization, that the way to improve schools is through even more centralized programs and regulations. For the last several years, their tool of choice has been the comprehensive, statewide reform plan, preferably in the form of a long, microscopically detailed law which is enacted by the state legislature and which imposes change from the top down. But it happens that this model violates nearly everything we know about effective schools. There has been an enormous amount of research on this subject over the last fifteen years, and the conclusions are strikingly consistent and strikingly harmonious with traditional common sense. The most effective schools are not necessarily those with the biggest budgets. But they are almost always those which enjoy strong leadership from the principal, a sense of teamwork among the faculty, and a climate of strong basic values shared by the school and the parents. These things cannot be

133

mass-produced by a centralized agency. In fact, the more power you transfer from local teachers and principals to the state capital, the harder it gets for schools to preserve the sense of responsibility and accountability that they need to be effective.

Thanks to all four of these mistaken assumptions, I believe that in the short term the reform movement has actually done more harm than good. For example, it became the principal vehicle for reversing the tax revolt of the 1970's, giving us tax increases in more than two-thirds of the states. These tax increases have had two practical effects: they have put more money into educational structures that are so overly centralized that they are inherently unworkable; and they have placed even heavier burdens on a social institution that is even more important than the schools, namely the family.

The reform movement *has* achieved some modest gains. It is now respectable once again to talk about "excellence," not just "equality"; educational programs are somewhat more likely to be judged by results, not claims. But test scores show that our schoolchildren continue to lag behind those of every other developed, civilized country. We are doing a somewhat better job of teaching minimal competency to the lowest-ability students, but the top five percent--our future leaders--are graduating from high school just as ignorant as they were before the reform movement took hold. Like it or not, measures like merit pay for teachers and courses in computer literacy don't even begin to address the core moral, philosophical and structural failings of the public-school monopoly. As time goes by, I think it will become increasingly clear that the principal effect of the 1980's reform movement was to distract attention from the only measures that might have worked: tuition tax credits and vouchers.

134

HIGHER EDUCATION IN A "DEMOCRACY OF WORTH": A PERSPECTIVE AND SOME PROPOSALS FOR RESTORATION

by Stephen M. Krason

There is a general belief in present-day America that education has deteriorated: other essays in this book present evidence of this decline. The lower levels of education generally follow the lead of higher education: the decadence which today characterizes elementary and secondary schools afflicted the higher learning first and continues to do so. While it is clear that much correction is necessary, theory must always precede practical proposals for change. This essay presents some beginning elements of a new theory which can help point the way to reconstruction, along with several specific proposals.

WHO SHOULD RECEIVE HIGHER EDUCATION?

Voices in America's past testify to the importance of education in a republic. Jefferson wrote to Madison: "Educate and inform the whole mass of people. Enable them to see that it is their interest to preserve peace and order and they will preserve them."[1] Madison himself stated: "Learned institutions ought to be favorite objects with every free people. They throw that light over the public mind which is the best security against crafty and dangerous encroachments on the public liberty."[2] DeTocqueville wrote:

> It cannot be doubted that in the United States the

135

> instruction of the people powerfully contributes to
> support the democratic republic. That will always be
> so, I think, where the instruction which teaches the
> mind is not separated from the education which is
> responsible for mores.[3]

While these eminent figures viewed the need for education as universal in a republic, they did not believe all citizens require the same type or level of education. Jefferson endorsed moral education[4] and a form of citizenship education in which those in a republic must be made to see that "it is in their interest to preserve peace and order."[5] He did not specify whether these should be carried out through formal schooling. Besides this, all citizens were to be provided an academic education in elementary schools to include the subjects of reading, writing, arithmetic, and geography. After this, "those destined for labor"--i.e., most people--would go to work in agriculture or enter apprenticeships in the handicraft arts. Only those who would be going into higher learning or the professions-- i.e., the future leaders of the political society--would "proceed to the college," which would consist of general schools and professional schools.[6] At this level, the really intense academic learning and broad study in the liberal arts would take place. Madison suggested that "primary schools" should be available to all,[7] but that higher levels of education should be supported primarily to "multiply the educated individuals, from whom the people may elect a due portion of their public agents of every description."[8] Higher schools for the purpose of shaping future leaders necessarily means their being limited to a minority. DeTocqueville's statement quoted above indicates that universal moral education is needed to make republican institutions secure. Moreover, he believed the education of most people in a republic "should be scientific, commercial, and industrial rather than literary." The study of the classics is only for the few "destined...to adopt a literary career or to cultivate such tastes."[9]

In short, the masses in a republic should receive an education in basic subjects and citizenship; the minority who will be the leaders require also advanced academic study in the liberal arts.

In today's terms, who would constitute the leadership group? In a society like ours, where significant activities are carried on not only by government but also the private sector, it clearly cannot mean only those who will go into politics or the government bureaucracy. It also includes those who will assume both major and minor policy- and decisionmaking tasks in such sectors of society as business, the press and media, religion, the legal profession, literature and the arts, education, the scientific community (including the medical profession), the military, and voluntary associations. Some of these fields, obviously, will require more advanced study than others.

Even though higher education need not--and, if it is to retain its standards, *should* not--be for everyone, in a democratic republic qualified persons should not be excluded from it. A sound basis for a theory of access to higher education in a democracy was put forth a generation ago by Philip H. Phenix. This theory has a moderate, realistic view which holds that education should be neither for the elite nor cater to the lowest mass tastes. An "exclusive, aristocratic type of education" which aims at producing "gentlemen" belonged in the type of society "where learning is a mark of freedom from the burdens of manual labor." The right type of democracy also excludes, on the other hand, the utilitarian idea of education geared primarily for "the pursuit of success and satisfaction through knowledge."[10]

What Phenix considers to be the right type of democracy is the one essentially endorsed by the Founding Fathers and deTocqueville. Phenix calls it the "democracy of worth." He defines it as "the social expression of belief in objective qualities of goodness and of common loyalty to them." It involves men seeking "ever fuller disclosure of the truth, through study, reflection, experiment, and dialogue, moved by shared devotion to...goodness." Education in a democracy of worth must thus stress "the habit of sustained inquiry and the arts of sincere persuasion, and above all should confirm and celebrate faith in the priority and ultimate givenness of truth and goodness..."[11]

The other, disordered type of democracy sees society as organized for "the greatest possible harmonization of desires." People in this type of democracy--the "democracy of desire"-- "strive only to get what they want," not to attain truth or goodness. The "common good" involves the maximizing of satisfaction and minimizing of conflict.[12]

A true "democratic education," according to Phenix, should be oriented to the truth--everyone must be viewed as being under the same ultimate authority of the truth. The primary goal of education must be to help everyone to gain knowledge which makes the truth more comprehensible, not to turn knowledge to their own private purposes or advantage. This is so regardless of whether these purposes or wants are those of individuals (as in a democracy of desire), a class (i.e., aristocratic "gentlemen"), or a whole society (i.e., when education primarily has the utilitarian purpose of promoting the objectives of the society or satisfying the expectations of mass opinion).[13]

Moreover, this supremacy of the truth means that not all beliefs or ideas can be held to be good or valid. The "democratic" nature of a democracy of worth consists not in the guarantee of an "equal hospitality to all beliefs" but in the "[o]penness to investigation of truth claims" (i.e., freedom of inquiry), the equal right of those who have the requisite ability to have access to the intellectual training which will permit them to take part in this investigation, and the equal obligation of all citizens to seek and uphold the truth.[14]

Phenix's theory translated into a practical policy for college and university admissions means, simply, that admission must be open to all citizens--so long as they meet the qualifications. The reasons why standards must be maintained in admissions are obvious: higher education is training the society's future leaders who will set the tone of its entire existence. If they are inefficient, incompetent, or ineffective, so will be the sectors of society they will lead. Further, if our leaders are not outstanding, the chances for maintaining our liberty and democratic traditions are lessened--as the Founding Fathers and deTocqueville knew--as are the possibilities of constructing Phenix's common good oriented to truth.

It would seem that such common practices in American higher education as "need" scholarships without regard to academic excellence, the admission of students with serious academic deficiencies (with the plan that remedial programs will be employed to correct them), and affirmative action or quotas in admissions--as well as in faculty hiring--are not in accordance with the principles just outlined. These practices make higher education appear to be a right which exists without regard to qualifications. They are typical of a democracy of desire in which people are given things merely because they want them.

I am well aware that federal and state laws and regulations make the reform of such practices difficult for many schools. If schools, especially private ones, really want to restore the standards associated with a democracy of worth, however, they could minimize government regulation by refusing financial assistance, student aid, and other programs from it.

A genuine desire to restore standards also requires that student recruitment practices be reevaluated. Probably no policy in recent times has done more to reduce the dignity of higher education than this. A democracy of worth requires that the high activity of pursuing the truth cannot be commercialized or huckstered. Recruitment is an activity which must be carried out with restraint and good taste. Schools should simply make a fair presentation of what they have to offer students, without "sales puffing" and through the proper mediums. Schools must place the interests of those they serve--students--ahead of their own enrollment projections. They should make clear to prospective students what is expected of them, even when they are simply inquiring about the school. They should be frank and prompt in telling them if they lack the ability, background, or qualifications to do well in their programs.

On this latter point, the issue involved--to use the frequently-heard phrase--is "excellence in education." What this demands in higher education is that students be expected to do *well*, not just get by as so many do. After all, our training of future leaders demands *high*, not minimal, standards.

STATE VERSUS PRIVATE HIGHER EDUCATION

The question of access to higher education raises the question of whether it is best provided by state or privately-controlled institutions. Clearly, the trend for this whole century has been toward greater reliance on the state to provide education at all levels and, where it does not actually provide it, to frame the terms within which the private sector will do so. The soaring cost of education in recent years has accelerated this trend.

There are a number of reasons why private higher education is preferable to that of the state. First, there is the problem of it violating a sound social ethics. The principle of subsidiarity--which finds a partial expression in the American democracy of worth in the principle of federalism--demands that government not assume tasks that can be effectively carried out by private efforts. The argument can at least be made--I shall not go into it further here--that this is the case with higher education. [15] Another reason is that state higher education tends to become increasingly bureaucratized and centrally controlled, so that those who traditionally have been in control of institutions--the faculty--have less and less say over them. Another is that when the state gets into an activity previously handled by the private sector it tends eventually to dominate it. We have seen this not only in education, but in social welfare, transportation, and other areas. Another problem is that politicians and the public want state institutions to secure access to their programs for more and more people. The result is an extraordinary pressure to lower standards. Even where states try to avoid this at their state university--by establishing community colleges, branch campuses and the like--the same result occurs: a greater number of students, many of whom lack the qualifications to do well, are enrolled in state higher education (even if at different locations). Another problem is that the relative financial security, even affluence, of state institutions (guaranteed by tax dollars) spoils them and causes them to have a false notion of what the educational enterprise really requires. They falsely insist that more and more buildings, laboratories, recreational facilities, and student service personnel are needed if learning is to be carried on properly. Finally, perhaps the greatest problem of state-controlled institutions of higher education is their secular environment, brought about by the state's judicially-mandated "neutrality" toward religion. One result of this "neutrality" has been to further encourage and give an official imprimatur to the ethical relativism which was already ascendant in most disciplines. All sorts of moral positions, no matter how depraved, are tolerated--both in the classroom and in student life on campus. Another result is that it is hardly acknowledged at most state universities that God is even a subject for serious intellectual inquiry or that there is a spiritual element to life at all. Both results make impossible the kind of education which Phenix's democracy of worth requires. As stated above, this education cannot treat all ideas and moral positions as equally valid; it must separate those which are true from those which are false. Truth and goodness--the objectives of

139

democratic education--cannot be achieved otherwise. Of course, education seeking the truth by definition must be concerned with ultimate questions and theology is the discipline which--with philosophy--is the most capable of dealing with them.

I do not suggest that all state institutions of higher education should be abolished. This is neither likely nor desirable. There are many state universities with outstanding academic reputations which are the homes of many first-rate scholars. What I would suggest is that efforts be made to shift our national perspective back to an acceptance of higher education as primarily a private responsibility (even though I am aware that declining academic standards, ethical relativism, and other problems also exist, in varying degrees, at virtually all private colleges and universities). Along with this should be a concerted effort by citizens and public officials to have the state reduce the scope of its involvement in higher education. The cause of democratic higher education, as I have discussed it, would be furthered if, for example, some of the commuity colleges, branch campuses, and former state teachers colleges were closed, turned over to private control, or else maintained at a smaller scale as vocational-technical institutes. In order to justify their continued existence, many function predominantly as vocational-technical or trade schools already. Some of the state funds used to maintain so many institutions could be turned into state grants to qualified students to permit them to attend private institutions.

SECULAR VERSUS RELIGIOUS INSTITUTIONS

Should higher education, ideally, be carried out by secular institutions--public or private--or those which have a religious affiliation? This could be the subject of a sizable essay itself; it can be treated only briefly here. Private non-sectarian institutions certainly are more able to conduct the serious inquiries into the ultimate questions than state-controlled ones, at least in theory, because they operate under no legally-mandated restrictions. In reality, however, they have ignored such inquiries almost as much as state institutions due to the prevalence of a radical, deep-seated secularist worldview. Religious institutions, or at least the small number which have not fallen prey to the same secularization, are clearly the most likely to motivate their students to think about first principles and transcendent truths. Their very nature insures this, even though sectarian doctrines and perspectives will result in differences in the way they conduct these inquiries and in the conclusions they derive.

This is not to say the private, non-sectarian schools cannot treat the ultimate questions as a true liberal education demands. One thinks of places like St. John's College in Annapolis and Santa Fe and individual departments and professors throughout the country which do this successfully. This can happen, however, only where militant secularism is not the reigning ideology or, at least, where true tolerance is practiced--which is the norm at a rapidly diminishing number of institutions. It is not likely, however, that the non-sectarian institution is equipped to stave off secularism in the long run because, like state institutions, it has no religious foundation. Sooner or later, to a greater or lesser degree, it is likely to become secularized. Since it does not rely on any body of religious principles or organize its institutional existence, it and the people connected with it will be shaped primarily by the secular culture around them. (Indeed, the modern private non-sectarian university is a development which parallels the phenomenon of secularization in Western society.) Moreover, even where non-sectarian schools *do* address ultimate questions, they do so inadequately because they do not go far enough. They tend to seek only naturalistic answers, which tendency is itself a reflection of secularism. They are reluctant to go too deeply into the theological issues for fear of wandering into sectarian doctrines. The denominational institutions, or at least those which identify themselves with a particular religious perspective (e.g., "Christian" colleges), do delve deeply into theology, of course, even if they do not all provide answers which contain the same amount of truth.

THE CONTENT OF HIGHER EDUCATION

The Liberal Arts and Career Preparation

An important aspect of any inquiry into the restructuring of higher education involves a consideration of what should be taught. Traditionally, of course, the answer to this at the undergraduate level (which will be the focus of my remarks) was the liberal arts. The belief that the liberal arts should be the cornerstone of the higher learning (i.e., the education provided in colleges and universities to the leadership group in society) is strongly defended in this essay. At the same time, it must be asserted that certain reasonable, but limited, modifications that have been made in most American college curricula in this century have been desirable. These include a movement away from the Greek and Roman Classics as the focal point for studies, especially in literature (although it has certainly been undesirable that the Classics have been pushed out of the picture almost entirely), an expansion of the number of areas of study brought under the heading of "liberal arts" and expected to be included in the undergraduate's program, and the introduction of the system of majors and pre-professional concentrations (e.g., pre-law and pre-medical). I view these changes as desirable because of the theory of access to higher education discussed above, the rise of the natural and physical sciences, the greater quantity and more technical character of knowledge, and the fact that the areas of intellectual endeavor that are important to the common good of a democratic republic today are so much more numerous than in the past. These points are discussed in this and the next subsection.

As Phenix has emphasized, education in a democratic republic cannot be exclusive; it cannot be restricted to the wealthy gentleman. Such exclusivity, besides going against our traditions, is also completely impractical in a society which depends so heavily on people from so many groups and backgrounds to keep it functioning. It is true that access to higher education can be extended to capable people of more modest means-- as Madison suggested would be appropriate in a democratic republic--by providing scholarships or other assistance.[16] This would hardly be adequate today, however, with the high cost of college education, a relatively limited amount of money that can be made available for scholarship funds (even when the state provides money for this), and the fact that simply more people need to be educated in a much larger society which relies more on the skills of the mind. Higher education thus must accommodate the young person who seeks first to gain an education for its own sake, but also has a career objective in mind. Students, or their parents paying for their education, who are not wealthy rightfully need to know that their substantial investment is likely to bring some kind of personal financial return in the future.

At the same time, higher education cannot become *primarily* education for a career because it would not properly train future leaders for a democracy of worth. To gain an appreciation of goodness and a belief in the truth and a commitment to securing a common good based upon that truth requires the traditional liberal learning. This seeks to rigorously train the mind, motivate the student to think critically and reflect on the ultimate questions, help him to see how the various fields of human knowledge complement each other to increase understanding, and liberate his mind from prejudices, ideological presuppositions, and provincialism which obscures the truth. To make a career the sole or even primary end of higher education is to direct it basically to the service of the individual student, to help him satisfy his wants. This is expected in a democracy of desire, but is not fitting for a democracy of worth.

Colleges and universities today, for the most part, still announce that they are committed to the above sort of relationship between the liberal arts and career preparation. College professors and administrators will frequently say it is their task to provide students who are primarily interested in being trained for a job in a particular field with a broad, humanistic education. What schools actually *do*, however, is often quite the opposite. They establish programs and departments--in some colleges and universities these predominate--to train students for highly technical and specialized fields (e.g., medical technology and criminal justice studies), drastically cut down the number of required courses in the humanistic disciplines, and promote themselves as, for example, providing the "job connection." While portraying themselves as maintaining a *balance* between liberal learning and career preparation--and perhaps *believing* they actually do this--they have really placed an extreme emphasis on the latter which has subverted the former.

This balance was maintained in the past by the system of majors and pre-professional concentrations. The undergraduate was able to get a broad liberal arts education while also beginning to carve out a specialty which gave him needed background for a job in his chosen field or for entry into professional school. The major and pre-professional courses were solidly academic in nature, which is not always the case with some specialty programs in colleges today. Their effect, in the final analysis, was simply to provide the student with more in-depth study in a selected area of the liberal arts. They did not *neglect* the liberal arts as is almost the case today.

The major system seems particularly appropriate for a democracy of worth. First, it is suited to a proper theory of access to higher education because it meets the needs of the majority of students (i.e., those who have career concerns). It gives them the opportunity to develop a specialty which a career demands. Second, it helps meet the needs of a modern post-industrial society confronted by a "knowledge explosion" by providing it with people who have gained a specialization in some intellectual area. The amount of knowledge today is so great that few people can be expected to acquire a mastery of it in more than one area; some degree of specialization simply is required. For a modern society to be able to channel and utilize the available knowledge is part of what conduces to its common good, which a democracy of worth aims for.

On the other hand, the major system was structured to preserve the broad, general learning of the liberal arts which is necessary to promote the good and the true, for both the individual and society, which are the other aspects of a democracy of worth. In short, it both helps to insure that higher education not become exclusive or impractical--the "democratic" part of a democracy of worth--and that it promote the things that make human and social life truly worth living--the "worth" part.

Modifications of the major system, such as "double-majoring," or the tendency of some schools to permit too many courses in the major create too much specialization and should be rejected. Such practices do not enable a student to get a sufficiently broad liberal arts education.

The Curriculum

Including more disciplines under the rubric of "liberal arts" requires a rethinking of curriculum. Obviously, it is not possible to dwell at length on this here; an entire book would be needed to give the subject the attention it deserves. The points that *will* be made concern the overall content of the curriculum and the place of the physical and natural sciences in the liberal arts.

If the purpose of a liberal education stated above are to be achieved, a curriculum needs to be devised which will enable the student to study and reflect upon the nature of man, his purpose and destiny, and his relationship to God, his fellow men, society, the natural moral order, and the physical universe. He must explore the nature of God and the moral order and gain an understanding of why they impose obligations on him. In order to answer questions about the human race of which he is part, a student must learn about its past. He must learn something about the nature of the physical universe if he is to understand man's relationship to it. This all suggests, in a general way, what disicplines should be included in a liberal arts curriculum: theology (involving man's relationship to God, man's purpose and his right conduct [as discerned from Revelation]): philosophy (logical thinking, man's purpose and right conduct [as discerned from natural reasoning alone]); history (man's past); literature and Classics (developing of the imagination through the creative use of language so we can better understand the relationships above and the dilemmas confronted by man in his existence[17]); foreign language studies (the same--when speaking about foreign literature--and also, simply, the easing of communication among men so there can be greater mutual insight into their cultures); the social sciences (the nature of men's cultures, their relationships in society, and their relationship to their political orders); the fine arts (also concerning the imagination and man's relationships, revealed in a different area of human creativity); and the physical and natural sciences (man's body--the physical dimension of his existence--and his relationship to the physical universe).

Moreover, a *smattering* of work in these various areas (e.g., with distributional requirements which give students wide leeway for choice) or a treatment of them which is too broad or unfocused (e.g., courses in "Western Civilization") will not accomplish the objective of the liberal arts. A commitment to truth means that the critical discipline of philosophy must be studied systematically and cumulatively. It means, for example, that a student must get a firm enough of an understanding of theology to be able to approach a knowledge of God. It means that he must read and study enough of the great works of literature to gain some understanding of how man saw himself in the major periods of world history. It also means that students do enough work in the above disciplines to see how each one complements the others' efforts in the quest for truth.

It is in this latter area particularly that studies in the Classics play an important role. I mentioned above that the contemporary curriculum is correct in deemphasizing the Greek and Roman Classics. I do not mean by this that the ancient writers are not a critical part of the curriculum, but only that it should not be built around them. The greatest of the works of the Classics should be learned because they provide some of the most penetrating insights into the human character and predicament and, because they represent the zenith in naturally-acquired truth about the nature of things, provide the measuring rod by which later ages are to be evaluated. There are great medieval and modern works of literature also, however, and the student must know them if he is to understand better why the world around him is as it is. If a truly educated modern man should know Thucydides, he should also know Chaucer, Shakespeare, and Charles Dickens. In taking this position, I basically endorse what I quoted deTocqueville as saying, but with modification. It is true that "literary education" is not for most people in a democratic republic because higher education is not for most people. As I have said, and as deTocqueville doubtlessly believed, it is only for future leaders. The modification occurs in the fact that this leadership group must be somewhat larger than his time required, that a liberal arts education now does not mean most basically a "literary" education, and that education in literature does not mean solely or even substantially the Classics. What the above *does* mean is that the Greek Books of various periods in literature and other fields, that Allan Bloom and others have touted so highly, should be an essential part of the liberal arts curriculum.[18] This does not imply that the Great Books should be the *sole* focus of the curriculum, however. A "Great Books curriculum" has its limitations. For example, how does one teach history or current American government in a coherent and complete way by using just the Great Books? Also, there are important commentaries on the Great Books and great authors which it can be worthwhile to expose students to.

I have no illusions about the likelihood of students today receiving the kind of training in philosophy--built around a study of the "perennial philosophy"--and theology which is needed. The influence of secularism and the inability of secular institutions to deal with the ultimate questions preclude such studies. This illustrates how closely the educational enterprise is tied to the philosophical and moral consensus of the society. If there is no consensus, acquiring a true liberal arts education becomes excruciatingly difficult and, by and large, cannot be done solely within the confines of a formal degree program.

The upshot of the above is that undergraduates need a common curriculum. In order for the same solid liberal arts background to be acquired by all students it is necessary that the curriculum, except for the part of it to be devoted to the major, be largely prescribed. Electives both make such a liberal education impossible and attribute to undergraduates a sagacity about their educational needs that few have. Moreover, there is another advantage of a common curriculum: it permits undergraduates at the same stage of their liberal arts education to study the same works together. This makes possible an association with each other on a common academic ground which is indispensable for the kind of intellectual give-and-take, inside the classroom and out, which characterizes a true liberal learning experience.

As a starting point for discussing science in the curriculum, we turn back to Phenix. He emphasizes the importance of adding new fields to the curriculum:

> If modern liberal education is to provide for the nurture of free men, it must regain the ideal of generality which characterized the traditional liberal arts, but it must do so without sacrificing the variety and scope made possible by modern advances in

145

knowledge.[19]

The physical and natural sciences fall into this category more clearly than any other (we might also include psychology here). They are obviously of great significance in our modern technological society and liberal education could not fully sustain its relevance if it did not make room for them. Upon acknowledging that these sciences have a place in the curriculum, two questions immediately present themselves: 1) Should every undergraduate be required to study them and, if so, how many of them and in what depth? and 2) Should they be offered as majors?

All undergraduates *should* have some study in the latter, although for those whose interest and concentration is in the humanities and social sciences it should be in the form of "science for the liberal arts" courses. Most will have already had some science study in secondary school. They should be required to take one or two courses in college which will enable them at least to learn what the basic, primary concepts in various sciences are (e.g., relativity in physics, the principles of Euclidean geometry, the subconscious in psychology) and about the history of science and the contributions made by the greatest scientists. They should also be required to consider questions about science--as, for that matter, should students majoring in the sciences--which can best be addressed by the other disciplines in the liberal arts, such as: In what ways has science had an impact on society? How has it affected our moral, social, and political attitudes and our perspective about ourselves? What role has it played in the rise of Western democracy? Which ethical approaches to the use of science and technology are most in keeping with the dignity of man?

Training for Those Entering the Sciences

I have little doubt that in our technological-industrial society--especially in light of what I have said about higher education accommodating career concerns and addressing national needs--undergraduates should be permitted to major in the basic sciences (i.e., biology, chemistry, geology, mathematics, psychology, and physics). I say "basic sciences" because these are theoretical in nature. The undergraduate science major should be concerned about gaining a solid theoretical grasp of his field to enable him to have the foundation either for more specialized studies in it or a closely related field or for one of the applied sciences. This means that "hybrid" sciences, such as biochemistry and biophysics, are best left for graduate study, as is work in certain engineering fields. The experience of institutions which have undergraduate programs in applied sciences such as engineering demonstrates that their extremely specialized focus and the intensity of study they demand is an obstacle to the student getting a broad liberal arts education. The number of courses required of science majors in their discipline should not be greater than for any other major. (It is understood that a few hours per week will have to be added to the normal course load for laboratory time.) Otherwise, the student majoring in science will not get the same strong liberal arts education as others.

Not every person interested in a career in a scientific field needs to receive a liberal arts education. Clearly, those who are planning to be biologists, chemists, psychologists, physicists, physicians, dentists and the like do. This is because they will be the *leaders* in the scientific and health care communities. Humane learning will help them to carry out their professions in a manner to be expected in a democracy of worth. The same would be the case for those in some engineering fields, but not all. A liberal arts education would seem to be indicated for those going into particular areas or specialties in engineering which involve policymaking affecting the public good. Special technical institutes or strictly engineering colleges would be sufficient for the others. Many of the health care professions which today are increasingly insisting on baccalaureate and even graduate degrees, such as physical therapy and nursing, would also be best prepared for in specialized, non-liberal arts schools. The reason, of course, that these professions and para-professions are insisting on a college degree is because they associate greater prestige with it. They have convinced state regulatory bodies that it is needed to insure more competent practitioners and thus greater protection for the public. Whether this actually has resulted is questionable. What *has* occurred has been, first, a lowering of college standards to accommodate all these students who really do not want and may not have the qualifications for liberal arts study and, second, a burgeoning of new "filler" courses in these fields, beyond the basic ones needed to master them, in order to give students enough credits in their majors to permit them to graduate.

LENGTH OF STUDIES

All this discussion of the curriculum presumes a four-year undergraduate program. I believe that this traditional length is desirable, even if I might be inclined to agree with Everett Dean Martin's view--expressed earlier in this century, but, I believe, still valid--that elementary-secondary education is simply too long.[20] At the college level, after all, we are training leaders who must emerge, above all else, knowing how to think and to exercise mature intellectual judgment. Developing this takes time, and four years is none too long. Moreover, the leap from secondary school studies to college is a quantum one: the materials studied are much more difficult and numerous and treated in a good deal more depth, at least in a college or university maintaining even minimal standards. The student needs time to digest and cogitate about them.

TEACHING, SCHOLARSHIP, AND ENROLLMENT SIZE

The foregoing discussion of the importance of curriculum should not deflect attention from the need for good teaching to insure a successful liberal arts experience. Serious students bent on getting a good liberal arts education often realize only in retrospect how vital a professor is and that they would have sometimes been better to "take the professor rather than the course."

As far as the attitude of institutions to teaching is concerned, much has been said and written about how many do not place enough emphasis on it and do not adequately reward good performance in it. As with the correction of many of the other problems in higher education which have been pointed to in this essay, this requires a change in attitude. Scholarship can no longer be seen as something restricted to--or, for that matter, necessarily demonstrated by--writing and publishing. Teaching, public speaking (not just before academic audiences), advising students on the right paths to take in their academic and personal lives (since education involves the "whole man"), service to the institution, and continual learning in one's field are activities which promote scholarship every bit as much as writing. Indeed, they are activities which may be *more* in accordance with the character of the true scholar than writing since they evidence humility and a willingness to serve others. This seems definitely to be what a democracy of worth requires from its scholars. Since such a democracy is characterized by, to repeat the above quote from Phenix, "the social expression of belief in objective qualities of goodness and of *common* loyalty to them," it is obviously a social phenomenon. It demands selflessness and service in order to further the truth.

Even good teachers can be handicapped by having to face large lecture halls jammed with students. This has been characteristic since World War II of what Russell Kirk has called "Behemoth U." and "Brummagem U."[21] This results from the mistaken belief that everyone should go to college and the desire to justify larger budgets with increased enrollments. If the "whole man" is to be educated--as liberal learning requires--the professor must get to know him personally. This is impossible without a manageable class size and, for that matter, a reasonable-sized college community.

A good size for undergraduate classes may well be only a dozen, certainly no more than twenty. Although there may be a place for tutorials and independent study on the undergraduate level, it is not appropriate, as it would be on the graduate level, to structure the program predominantly in this manner. Undergraduates need lecturing and also the opportunity for intellectual give-and-take with classmates. Correspondingly, the ideal size of an undergraduate college may well be around 350 students. This size makes it feasible for dedicated faculty members to really get to know their students and take an active part in their lives outside of the classroom, to provide help and guidance in both their academic and personal development.

It is true that the diversity and greater resources afforded by a large university can be an advantage in a student's educational development.[22] One's perspectives are always broadened by meeting individuals from different backgrounds and from different parts of the country or world, as is more likely to occur at a mega-university than a very small college. There is no guarantee, however, that this benefit will be derived by the student at the former. Most of the other students in his classes may be similar to him and he may simply not have the occasion to meet many of the interesting array of people who pass by him on the campus sidewalks or corridors. If he does meet them, he may not get to know them well enough for them to leave an impression on him. Moreover, there may be other ways for him to make up for this lost "advantage" (e.g., travel abroad, exchange programs). The wide diversity of course offerings found at the large school is not really an advantage, as my discussion indicates. What the undergraduate needs is a strong grounding in the basic humanities, social sciences, and physical/natural sciences and an education in the important books which have shaped our culture. This demands a largely prescribed curriculum. As far as resources are concerned, the key element is library holdings. The more limited holdings of the small college are usually adequate for undergraduates who buy most of their books for courses and do not carry on the extensive research graduate students do.

Of course, we are not likely to see established colleges and universities reverting to this scale anytime soon. This is probably most closely approximated in very small colleges, particularly those of a denominational cast which have not become secularized or have recently been established in reaction to such secularization. On the latter point, new Catholic institutions like Thomas Aquinas College, Christendom College, Magdalen College, and The Thomas More College of Liberal Arts come to mind.

While I believe the establishment of new institutions such as these is to be encouraged--in order both to help restore sound liberal arts training and provide education at a manageable scale--there has been a hopeful, though limited, development in the older universities with the creation of new institutes and programs to provide a traditional liberal arts curriculum to a limited number of students. Examples are the Integrated Humanities Program (formerly Pearson College) at the University of Kansas, the St. Ignatius Institute at the University of San Francisco, the Program of Liberal Studies at the University of Notre Dame, and the Center for Christian Wisdom at Gannon University. It is doubtful, however, that these are a trend and such entities often have come under intense pressure from within their universities. I do not believe that the increasing tendency of universities to reinstitute watered-down general education requirements is even a half-step in the right direction.

STUDENT DISCIPLINE

Another factor besides class and college size which contributes to a good learning environment--which is essential for a good liberal education experience--is the maintenance of student discipline.

Student discipline, except where it has involved destruction of property,

149

egregious acts of classroom disruption, or a direct assault upon the integrity of the academic activity--as by cheating or plagiarism--(and sometimes not even in these cases), has been something which university administrations for some years have almost ignored. This is because they see education as involving only academics and not also character; they are oblivious to the need to educate the "whole man." The ultimate reason for this--their unwillingness to be concerned about normative matters because they do not believe truth is attainable--is discussed perceptively in John S. Schmitt's essay in this book (this outlook certainly characterizes higher education in the same way as the elementary-secondary education he specifically focuses on). Apart even from this, however, their inattention to disciplinary matters undercuts their very efforts to provide students with a strong academic education. Academics requires discipline and if a student is not disciplined in other areas of life, why should we expect him to be in his academic work? The belief of many educators that facts can be separated from values also leads them to believe that the human being is truncated: he can somehow have an intellectually ordered life when the rest of his life is disordered.

The principle that university and college administrations have followed on student discipline for the last twenty-five or so years is to permit the utmost freedom in matters of "personal" morality (e.g., alcohol, drugs [at least "soft" drugs], religious observance, and, especially, sex). The result has been that schools turn out graduates who have skills for jobs, but no ability to engage in responsible and truly civilized living. They may go on to successful careers, but their personal lives are frequently marked by turmoil and unhappiness. Can it honestly be said that a higher learning which follows such a course is giving the student what he needs as a *person* (which is, after all, its purpose)?

Further, we must recall deTocqueville's words about how American education provided training for mores, as well as the mind. In doing so, it helped create the conditions which made it possible to sustain a democratic republic. Thus, if educators do not concern themselves with student discipline and proper character formation, they are not carrying out a vital aspect of their role in our society, and, in fact, are directly contributing to the society's decline.

To create an environment, by the lack of disciplinary rules, where students are permitted and are even encouraged to give in to their desires is not conducive to a democracy of worth where self-satisfaction must give way, *in all areas of life*, for the sake of the common good focused on truth. A democracy of worth demands that judgments be made about right and wrong beliefs and behaviors and that those which are right be pursued.

What colleges and universities *need* to do is to start viewing themselves once again as having the responsibility to act *in loco parentis* and take student discipline seriously. There are indications that there is a slight movement in this direction. Colleges have begun to address the problem of student alcohol abuse and they see themselves as acting in somewhat of an *in loco parentis* role in dealing with fighting and other serious misconduct between students.

It is unpopular to say this today, but I believe coeducation played a definite role in eroding student discipline and lessening the attention paid to academics. It results in social life becoming a greater distraction for students. Kirk speaks about "the dating-and-mating pattern which obsesses the typical American campus,"[23] and we are all familiar with the phenomenon of young people going to college primarily to find spouses. Also, in an increasingly secularistic and morally relativistic atmosphere, the temptations to premarital sexual activity became greater, as did the concommitant problems of out-of-wedlock births and abortion among college women. The once semi-monastic character of the American college has been radically transformed, especially since the 1960s.

With coeducation apparently here to stay, the universities and colleges should deal with its undesirable effects as best they can. This would mean adopting such former practices and policies as single-gender dormatories without visitation privileges, genuine dorm supervision (by non-peers), stern disciplinary measures for sexual misconduct, dress restrictions so as to insure the prevalence of modesty and good taste, the encouragement of wholesome social activities, and cooperation with religious groups in their campus efforts (at least by making it as easy as possible for them to do their work). I am well aware that the established secularized institutions, pushed to maintain coeducation by feminist ideology and government mandates and to tolerate wayward student sexual conduct by the prevailing moral relativism, are unlikely to go along with these proposals. They, however, are what must be done if the proper student discipline is to prevail. This is all the more reason why the established colleges and universities may be unable any longer to truly and completely educate young people.

CONCLUSION

This essay has attempted to establish a framework for considering what the nature of higher education should be like in a democracy of worth, the kind of political-social order which traditionally characterized America. It has considered various important questions, such as what the purpose of higher education in a democracy of worth is, who should receive it, what type of institutions are best able to provide it, what conditions must be met to provide it well, and what kind of curriculum is necessary. I do not believe that most of the perspective and proposals put forth are likely to be adopted by the established colleges and universities in the foreseeable future. This would involve a changed perspective on fundamental questions which go beyond educational views to philosophical, moral, and social considerations, which at the present time is highly unlikely among the members of the mainstream intelligentsia. If they *are* to be brought to fruition anywhere, it, for the most part, with certain exceptions, would have to be in new institutions which are unencumbered by the ideological baggage of the present-day and wish to carry on an idea of education firmly rooted in the traditions of our nation and our civilization.[24]

NOTES

1. Jefferson correspondence to Madison, Dec. 20, 1787, in Koch, Adrienne & Peden, William, eds., *The Life and Selected Writings of Thomas Jefferson.* N.Y.: Modern Library, 1944, p. 440.

2. Madison correspondence to W.T. Barry, Aug. 4, 1822, in Padover, Saul K., ed., *The Forging of American Federalism: Selected Writings of James Madison.* N.Y.: Harper & Row, 1953, p. 313.

3. DeTocqueville, Alexis, *Democracy in America.* (J.P. Mayer, ed.) Garden City, N.Y.: Doubleday (Anchor), 1969, Vol. One, Pt. II, p. 304.

4. Jefferson correspondence to Thomas Law, Esq., June 13, 1814, in Koch & Peden, p. 639.

5. Jefferson correspondence to Madison, Dec. 20, 1787, in Koch & Peden, p. 440.

6. Jefferson correspondence to Peter Carr, Sept. 7, 1814, in Koch & Peden, p. 642.

7. Madison correspondence to Thomas W. Gilmer, Sept. 6, 1830, in Padover, p. 315.

8. Madison correspondence to W.T. Barry, Aug. 4, 1822, in Padover, p. 313.

9. DeTocqueville, Vol. Two, Pt. I, pp. 476-477.

10. Phenix, Philip H., *Education and the Common Good.* N.Y.: Harper & Row, 1961, p. 38.

11. *Ibid*, p. 7.

12. *Ibid*, pp. 7-8.

13. *Ibid.*, pp. 38-39.

14. *Ibid.*

15. The principle of subsidiarity is defined and explained well in Dr. Water's essay in this volume. Waters indicates that, by and large, the development of public education, at least at the elementary and secondary levels, in countries like the U.S. has occurred in violation of this principle.

16. See Madison correspondence to W.T. Barry, *op. cit*, pp. 313-314.

152

17. This characterization of liberature is based in part on the description of it in the 1983-85 *Catalogue of the Thomas More Institute* (now College) *of Liberal Arts*, p. 14.

18. See Bloom, Allan, *The Closing of the American Mind: How Higher Education Has Failed Democracy and Impoverisihed the Souls of Today's Students.* (N.Y.: Simon & Schuster, 1987), pp. 344-347.

19. Phenix, p. 116.

20. Martin, Everett Dean, *The Meaning of a Liberal Education.* Garden City, N.Y.: Garden City Pub. Co., 1926, p. 73.

21. See Kirk, Russell, *Decadence and Renewal in the Higher Learning.* South Bend, Ind.: Gateway, 1978, *passim.*

22. See Tonsor, Stephen J., "Two Cheers for Behemoth University," in *Modern Age*, Vol. 23, No. 2 (Spring 1979), pp. 123-129, for a number of arguments in defense of the large university, as against the small liberal arts college, as being the preferable place for undergraduate education.

23. Kirk, p. 306.

24. One exception to this generalization is my own Franciscan University of Steubenville, an "established" Catholic university which has put a significant part of the perspective and proposals outlined in this essay into effect--with the promise that even more will be put in place in the future--as part of a profound transformation--due to the increasing seriousness with which it has viewed its religious commitment--which has occurred in the overall character and direction of the institution in recent years.

INDEX

ABOUT THE CONTRIBUTORS

Dr. John Agresto is President of St. John's College in New Mexico and was formerly Vice Chairman of the National Endowment for the Humanities.

John S. Schmitt is Headmaster of Trivium School in Lancaster, Massachusetts.

Dr. Raphael T. Waters is Associate Professor of Philosophy at Niagara University.

The Reverend J. Donald Monan, S.J., Ph.D. is President of Boston College.

Dr. Russell Kirk is a prominent lecturer on education, editor, and man of letters who has authored over twenty books.

Dr. David Lowenthal is Professor of Political Science at Boston College.

Dr. Christopher Bruell is Professor of Political Science at Boston College.

The Honorable William M. Bulger is President of the Senate of the Commonwealth of Massachusetts.

Dr. Ralph Lerner is Professor of Social Sciences in the College of the University of Chicago.

Dr. Peter V. Sampo is President of The Thomas More College of Liberal Arts in New Hampshire.

Dr. Richard H. Powers in Professor of History at the University of Massachusetts at Boston.

Annette Kirk was a member of the National Commission on Excellence in Education.

Lawrence A. Uzzell is an editoral writer for Scripps-Howard newspapers and former President of LEARN, Inc., a Washington, D.C.-based think tank on education.

Dr. Stephen M. Krason, Esq. is Associate Professor of Political Science at Franciscan University of Steubenville and was formerly Eastern Director of the Intercollegiate Studies Institute.